Table of Contents

List of Figures

THE SPANISH PIONEERS IN UNITED STATES HISTORY

THE MELUNGEONS: The Pioneers of the Interior Southeastern United States 1526-1997

By

Eloy J. Gallegos

Villagra Press
Knoxville, Tennessee
1997

Published by Villagra Press,
2301 Clinch Avenue, Knoxville, TN 37916

Library of Congress Catalog Card Number: 97-61691

ISBN Number: 1-882194-32-2

Cover Design and Illustrations:
Stephen E. Gallegos: Atlanta, Georgia

Other books by Eloy Gallegos:

Jacona
An Epic Story of The Spanish Southwest

The Spanish Pioneers In United States History
Santa Elena
Spanish Settlements on the Atlantic Seaboard
from Florida to Virginia 1513 to 1607

Spanish Pioneers In United States History
El Quartelejo
Home-Far-From-Home

Introduction

A few years ago in late Fall of 1990, after the trees had shed their leaves and the rattlesnakes and copperheads had retired for the winter, I ventured into the deep woods of Polk County in southeastern Tennessee. I went in search of the remains of an old fort, a fort whose origins have been shrouded in mystery. The blockhouse which had been a later addition to the original fort presently sits by the roadside outside Benton, Tennessee. The Benton site is the third place of residence for the blockhouse. I went in search of the original site. I was reasonably certain it lay along a small creek very appropriately labeled Old Fort Creek. The creek crossed the Old Federal Road a few miles north of the Conasauga River close to the Georgia-Tennessee state line.

During the course of the morning, I made several inquiries of people living along the Old Federal Road which parallels US 411 in southwestern Polk County, Tennessee. Ultimately I was referred to an octogenarian, tall, gaunt, dark, with a face that could have been the face of some of my uncles in Northern New Mexico. According to my referent, he was pure Cherokee or so he claimed when asked to explain his dark features. His cottage stood on the banks of Old Fort Creek (he did not know the name of the creek), and his cottage was barely visible from the road a mere forty feet distant, the kudzu vines having completely overrun the trees and tall bushes running along the road's perimeter. He knew where the site of the old fort was located, however, it was the second location of the blockhouse with which he was most familiar. It was directly across the creek from his cottage in a low place also engulfed by kudzu vines. The original location according to him was farther upstream atop a tree-covered rise on the left. He indicated that he had never been there himself.

The location of the fort site became secondary momentarily as I looked in the hazel eyes of a man who could have passed for a resident of any isolated mountain village in present-day Northern New Mexico. He had a classic "Spanish face," one with which I was very familiar having grown up in one of those remote Spanish villages in the Southwestern United States. I was looking into the eyes of a man whose own ancestors had lived in isolation in the Southeastern United States for more than fifteen generations. I have looked into thousands of such faces in every Southeastern state and in several Midwestern and Western states including South Central Canada. I was certain that he was a Melungeon, however, during my fifteen year search for the origins of those isolates known as Melungeons, I had learned that the term "Melungeon" brought forth varied emotional reactions. As we sat easy-like on his front stoop, he sat on a no-back bench pushed against the wall and I on the top step of the plank steps looking into his worn, wrinkled face. Behind to his right I could also catch a glimpse of the hazy upthrust of the Smoky Mountains. We spoke easily about a variety of topics. I was hoping to ease him into talking about his heritage. I related to the experiences of my own people in Northern New Mexico prior to the Second World War. I informed him that my heritage took me back fifteen generations to the time when my ancestors had come to the Kingdom of New Mexico in 1598 to settle, and they had lived in isolation in those remote parts of the mountainous West much like a mysterious people of the Southeastern United States had lived and struggled. These people, the Melungeons, I informed him were the first European pioneers to settle in Tennessee, Virginia, Kentucky, North Carolina, South Carolina, Georgia and Alabama, yet all they had to show for their efforts was persecution.

I focused on his eyes when I mentioned the term "Melungeon." His eyes flashed for an instant, and he jerked his shoulders back against the porch wall. He looked intently at me for a long time.

Neither one of us spoke until finally he looked directly at me and asked, "Are you one of those people?"

My reply to him was, "No, I am not a Melungeon, but I come from the same roots, and I have experienced similar experiences due to prejudice and ignorance. Our roots are of those valiant Spanish pioneers who came to Southeastern and Southwestern United States from Northern Spain and Portugal almost four hundred and fifty years ago to settle in the hopes of a better life. I am not one of them (Melungeons), but I honor and respect them for their courage and strength."

He sat stiffly for a few minutes, quietly nodding his head. Finally in a low quavering voice he stated, "I am one of those people. I am a Melungeon." He paused momentarily continuing to look me straight in the eye as he asked, "Who are we? You know who you are, but mine are still forgotten people. What is our heritage?"

A people who do not know who they are and from whence they came cannot walk side by side with pride with one who knows the achievements of his predecessors.

Eloy J. Gallegos
August, 1997
Knoxville, Tennessee

Part I
THE HISTORY—LUCAS VASQUEZ DE AYLLON

I

The heritage of Southeastern Isolates, primarily the Melungeons, embodies the struggle for existence of men, women and children who have clung for centuries to a precarious foothold in a climate of hate and intolerance. Their heritage left us a people who have spanned the gap of time in a humble yet relentless day-by-day mode of survival in that lonely place between the light and dark races.

These people were the first European settlers of four of the original thirteen colonies, Virginia, North Carolina, South Carolina and Georgia. In addition, they were also the first European settlers of Tennessee, Kentucky and Alabama. The first pioneers to come to settle came to Virginia and/or North Carolina in 1526 eighty years before the English Jamestown Colony and almost one century before the Pilgrims in present-day Massachusetts. Forty years later soldier/settlers in greater numbers arrived in the interior of Georgia and South Carolina. Incredible as it may seem, more than fourteen generations later the blood of these early Spanish pioneers still flows in tens of thousands of isolates called Melungeons, Lumbees, Red Bones, Brass Ankles and Turks.

The 1526 arrivals came to present-day North Carolina and Virginia to the Albemarle Sound and Chesapeake Bay vicinity in company with Lucas Vasquez de Ayllon, an educated man, a Judge, a non-military man. As the chronicler, Oviedo, stated in his historia, "I knew him well. Never did he dress in armor nor with sword so as to gain profit from it."

Ayllon cleared the Port of La Plata in Hispanola sometime during the middle of July, 1526, with one large ship, which was his flagship, and another called the Bretona, and another named Santa Catalina, and another called Chorruca, and a brigantine and a tender or barge. There totaled six vessels in all carrying five hundred men and women with most of the men being skilled in their trade including clergy, craftsmen, and medical personnel.[1] One of the members of the clergy was Fray Antonio Montesino who in earlier years had defied the civil authorities of the Indies by openly preaching and protesting the poor treatment of the Indians by some Spaniards. On board also were eighty to ninety fine horses, and large quantities of provisions and food supplies.

Ayllon's fleet sailed northerly from La Plata, on the island of Hispanola and made landfall at the mouth of a large river located on thirty-three degrees forty minutes.[2] The head pilot of the fleet was the same Pedro Quexos who had sailed north for Matienzo in 1520 and later switched his allegiance to Lucas Vasquez. Pedro Quexos was off the mark if he was attempting to strike land at a familiar landing place, the San Juan Bautista (Santee). Instead of reaching the San Juan at about thirty-three degrees latitude, he made landfall at Cabo Romano (Cape Fear) thirty-five degrees latitude as specified in his contract with the King as being the southern most line below which Ayllon was authorized to settle. Being unfamiliar with the entrance to this particular river and in all probability assuming that it was the San Juan Bautista, the Spaniards struck the sand bar at the entrance with the flagship, and it promptly sank taking with it most of its precious cargo. The people on board at the time, however, were rescued, and not one life was lost. The other ships being smaller and drawing less draught were able to negotiate entrance to the river without mishap. On discovering that this was a newly discovered river they promptly named it the Jordan, present-day Cape Fear River. So as not to burden the remaining ships with the salvaged cargo of the sunken flagship, Ayllon immediately commenced construction of another vessel. It was a small vessel made in the form of a gabarra (lighter) which the Spaniards appropriately named Gabarra. It is noteworthy to call attention to this event as the first instance of shipbuilding on the Atlantic Seaboard.

While the shipbuilding was in progress, some of the captains among the colonists explored the interior and returned with news that it was unsuited for establishing themselves on it. Additionally, the ships went ahead cautiously along the coastline above and returned with the good news of having found a more suitable land. In the meantime, Ayllon's trusted Indian slave, Francisco Chicora, saw his opportunity to escape, and he did so taking the other interpreters with him leaving Ayllon unable to communicate with the inhabitants. There is no mention made by the chroniclers of any significant Indian activity at this particular place as it is quite possible that the Indians, not unlike the Spaniards, also found it unsuitable. On receiving the news of a more suitable land ahead (adelante)[3], the Spaniards celebrated much, being that they were discontented with the spot where they were and also with the lack of Indian interpreters.

Immediately, they transported the women and the ill by ship, and the soldiers and men and presumably the horses went by land and eventually they all met at San Miguel de Guandape (Gualdape) which was the good land which they had earlier reconnoitered. It was estimated to be between forty and fifty leagues more distant toward the north. Since San Miguel was not shown on any map of that time, it was not known with any degree of certainty where it was located except that it was north of Cabo Trafalgar (Cape Hatteras) as indicated by the historians, Herrera, Oviedo, Navarette and Gomora.[4] And it certainly had to be beyond this point since Cape Hatteras is immediately above 35 degrees latitude and the asiento (royal contract with the king) stated 35, 36, and 37 degrees.

During late Spring of 1525 Quexos reconnoitered the Atlantic Seaboard as high as 39 degrees 40 minutes north. Consequently, Ayllon was familiar with the seacoast which lay between 35 degrees and 37 degrees. The Ayllon people were aware of Pamlico and Albemarle Sound, and the inlets leading into it from the Atlantic. One such inlet (not named) lay immediately north of Cabo Trafalgar (Cape Hatteras). Chaves called the body of water inside the barrier islands Bahia de Santa Maria, a name that was later given to Chesapeake Bay also.[5]

It is unlikely that Ayllon, being a judge of the Royal Audiencia and having knowledge of the law, would have established himself south of 35 degrees. By doing so he would have violated the royal contract thereby forfeiting all royal grants and privileges. By locating himself and his settlers below 35 degrees, Ayllon would have intruded on lands which were within the two hundred league buffer zone between royal grants. Juan Ponce's northernmost point was the 30 degree line of latitude, and it is approximately two hundred leagues from the 30 degree line to the 35 degree line of latitude in the proximity of Cabo Trafalgar. The fact that Juan Ponce was deceased did not free his grants to others as his son fell heir to his father's grants. The site of the Ayllon settlement did not come to light until 1609 almost eighty-five years later when Francisco de Ecija's spy mission out of San Agustin located the place where the English had had their settlement. On two separate occasions, Indians in the region along Cape Fear informed Ecija that San Miguel de Guandape was between forty and fifty leagues overland toward the north from the Cape Fear vicinity across the Llanos de San Roman. They further informed him that the English had been a few days journey from Guandape.[6] This would have placed San Miguel somewhere at the head of Albemarle Sound on the Roanoke River. Obviously, the place (a large island completely surrounded by water) where the English had been settled refers to Roanoke Island and Raleigh's colonies of the middle 1580's. This location also fits the 40 to 45 leagues given by the Spanish historians of that time as being the distance traveled from Cabo Romano (Cape Fear) to San Miguel well within the 35 and 37 degrees of latitude.[7]

Immediately upon arriving at San Miguel, the Spaniards commenced building houses since there were no Indian houses or huts on the site or in close proximity and winter was fast approaching. The land was at the selected site close to a river and there were many swamps. The river was copious and abounded with fish. Its entrance was low and difficult to navigate, and only with the tide from the sea could ships negotiate entrance across the sand barrier protecting Albemarle Sound from the heavy seas of the Atlantic.[8] The abundance of fish was noted by the colonists and some of those who survived the ill-fated expedition as they related later to the historian Oviedo who wrote in his *HISTORIA* that the colonists took in one channel over seven hundred flounders, and some to them much superior than those of Spain. Many other types of fish were also taken at different times, i.e. whitings, marine crabs, sea bream of one span (eight inches) of length. But among other than those above were many longer-eels, dogfish, sharks big and small, and good crowfoots. There were two fish of which Oviedo tells us were much marveled at by the Spaniards. One was a shark so large that the Justice of the Peace ordered that it not be eaten. However, in spite of his warning, four or five men ate of it, and shortly after having done so, all of their body hair fell off

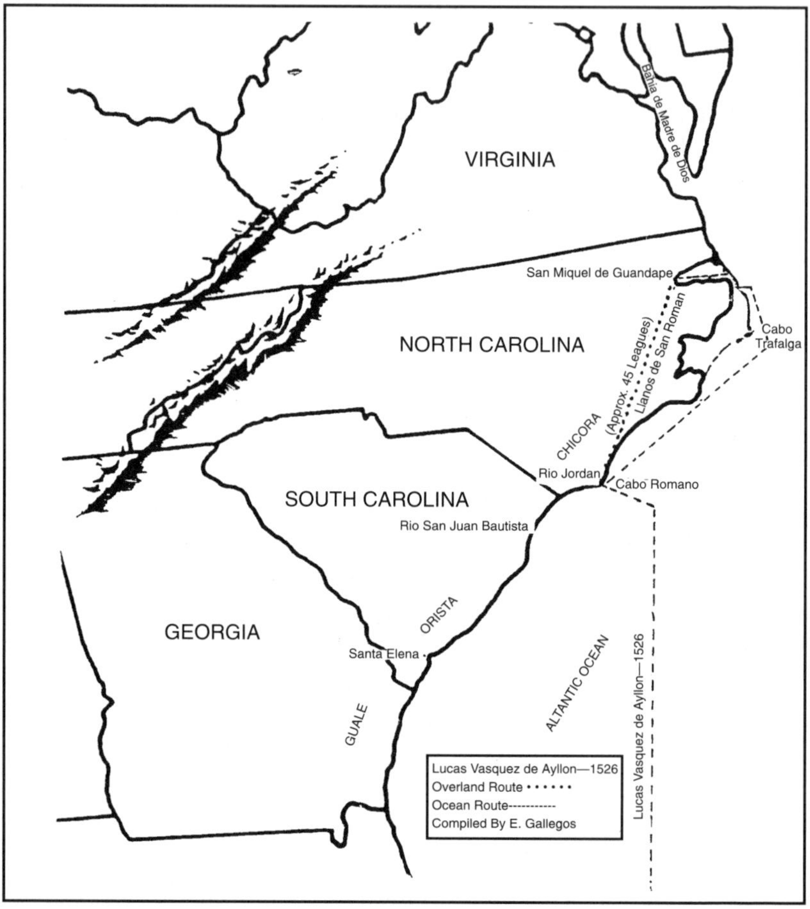

Figure 1. SAN MIGUEL DE GUANDAPE

including their beards and eye brows. As Oviedo reports, "Nor in any other parts of their bodies there remained any hair."[9]

The other remarkable fish was one denizen of the sea that had a shell like a turtle, but was like the one of crawfish and black. It had many feet on each side or flank and on opening it the Spaniards found many eggs no bigger than lentils. While raw, this fish and its eggs smelled much like mollusk and when cooked it smelled very good, and it was a delicacy and good for digestion. Of the native people and their culture, Oviedo relates that the entire coastline from the River of Santa Elena (should be Jordan) which is on about 33 degrees 30 minutes up to and around Cabo Trafalgar and on to the River of Guandape (Albemarle Sound/Roanoke River) is all level land and that there are few Indian settlements along that stretch of sandy coastline. The few that exited were of great distance one from the other; however, on some small islands off the coast the villages were small. In the villages there were mosques or temples of the idolatrous Indians. Also in the villages were charnel houses or family vaults of the common people where bones of the dead were kept. The houses or temples had walls of rough stone and mortar (lime made with oyster shells), and they were at least one estado (1.85 yards) and a half in height. Above the stone walls one estado in height rose the remainder of the walls constructed of lumber from pines, of which there are many in those parts.[10]

In addition to the mosques or temples, there were principal or communal houses. They were usually large and made of very tall and graceful pine trees that were limbed by the natives their entire height except for the very tops where the pruners left branches and leaves. The trees were aligned closely side-by-side into two rows fifteen to thirty feet apart which in essence formed two walls of trees. The length of each row of trees measured well more than three hundred feet and the tops of the trees were joined together, thereby forming a skeletal protective covering inside the two top rows of trees. Matting was then woven in and around the skeletal frame enveloping the entire area under the outer rows of pine trees, except for special openings used to draw out the smoke from the cooking fires. Cross-way from each of the outer rows of pine trees was another row of trees inside the compound in close proximity to the outer wall. In this manner was affected a double thickness of tree walls which made the communal houses strong, relatively well sheltered and defensible. In each of these long houses lived as many as two hundred people with each family having its own private entrance as desired.[11] These communal houses were not unlike the "long houses" of the Iroquois which is not coincidental since some of the Indian tribes along this stretch of the Atlantic coastline and into the interior for some distance were of Iroquoian linguistic stock.

Of the animals, birds, trees, and herbs, Oviedo relates in his *HISTORIA*, accounts that the surviving members of the colony which returned to Hispanola passed on to him. The animals included tigers, (mountain lions), tapirs or American tapirs, stags, rabbits, jackals, (that were like foxes and many of them were very mottled and screamed all the night without stopping until the coming day begins to dawn), wild cats, gray squirrels with only two upper teeth with which they pierce walnuts and eat the insides which are very difficult to separate from the shell.

The trees that the colonists informed Oviedo existed in that land were pines, oaks which yielded gall-nuts, evergreen oaks of acorns, vines of montigenous grapes, chestnuts (but the fruit was small), willows, cane like that of Spain, walnut trees, blue berries used for making raisins which the Indians dried and saved for winter. There were black mulberry trees and laurels, many sumach trees and good dwarf fan-palm like those of Spain.[12]

Although the colonists made substantial progress during the late summer and early fall of 1526, winter caught them unprepared. The loss of the flagship and most of its precious cargo earlier that summer off the coast of Cabo Romano (Cape Fear) left them desperately short of provisions. With the approaching winter season and its cold bitter winds many of the colonists became ill and died of the pestilent fevers common to the low lying swamps. Others died of hunger and cold. This scene must have been reminiscent of the English colonists at Jamestown who also perished of fevers, cold and hunger almost eighty-five years later on a spot very similar to the location of San Miguel where Spanish colonists struggled and died in 1526 in search of a better life. Even though there was a great abundance of fish in the rivers and animals in the forests, once the cold weather arrived at Bahia de Santa Maria (Albemarle/Pamilico Sounds) most of the colonists were too weak from illness to obtain food by that manner.

One of those who died of the pestilent fever was *El Licenciado* Lucas Vasquez de Ayllon, Governor of lands shown on later maps as Tierra de Ayllon. Ayllon succumbed on the Feast day of San Lucas on the 18th day of October of the year of 1526.[13] *El Licenciado* died like a Catholic, having received the Sacraments and repentant of his faults and sins. Before he died, Lucas Vasquez made arrangements for the continued administration of his foundling colony. In his place as governor, he ordered his nephew, Juan Ramirez, who at that time was treasurer of the Island of San Juan and presently resided on the island, be appointed governor and serve in that capacity at such a time when Ramirez could journey to San Miguel de Guandape. Until that time though so matters could progress within the settlement, Ayllon ordered that his captain and deputy, Francisco Gomez, assume immediate command. Gomez, however, was unable to govern as ably as Ayllon had, and it was not long before certain disorderly, belligerent mutineers emerged causing trouble and unrest.

The principal mutineer was one Gines Doncel, resident of Santo Domingo, Hispanola but native of Gibraltar. The other

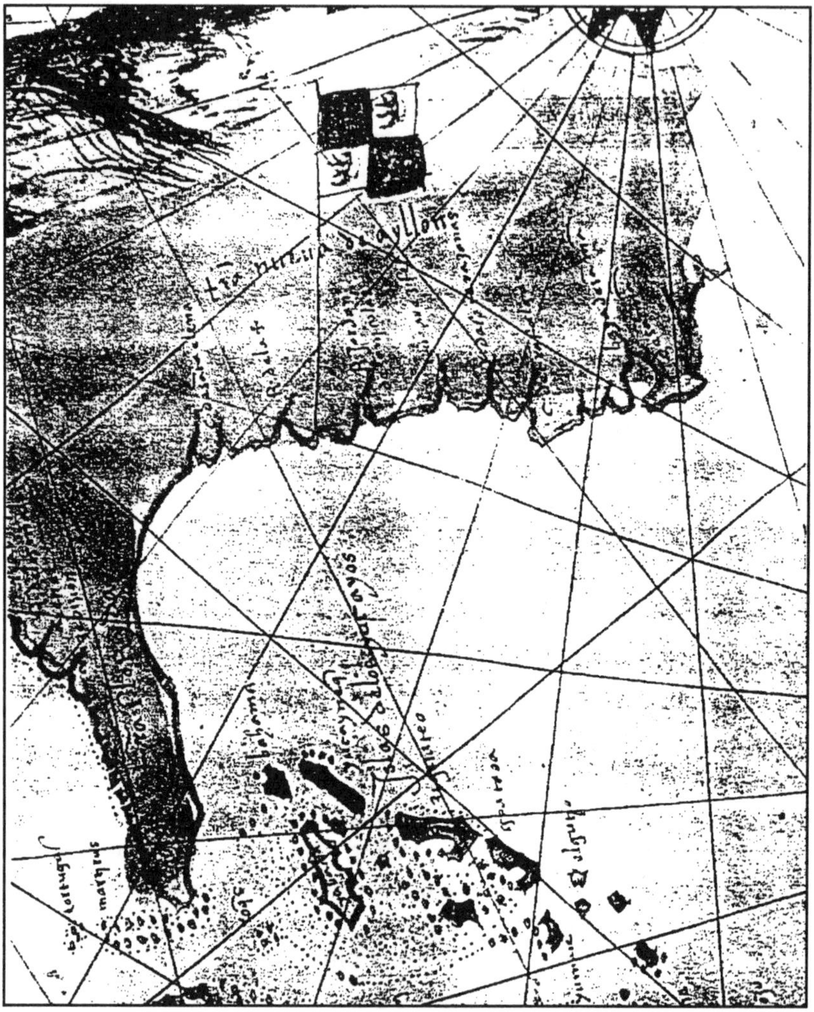

Figure 2. JUAN VESPUCCI MAP—1526

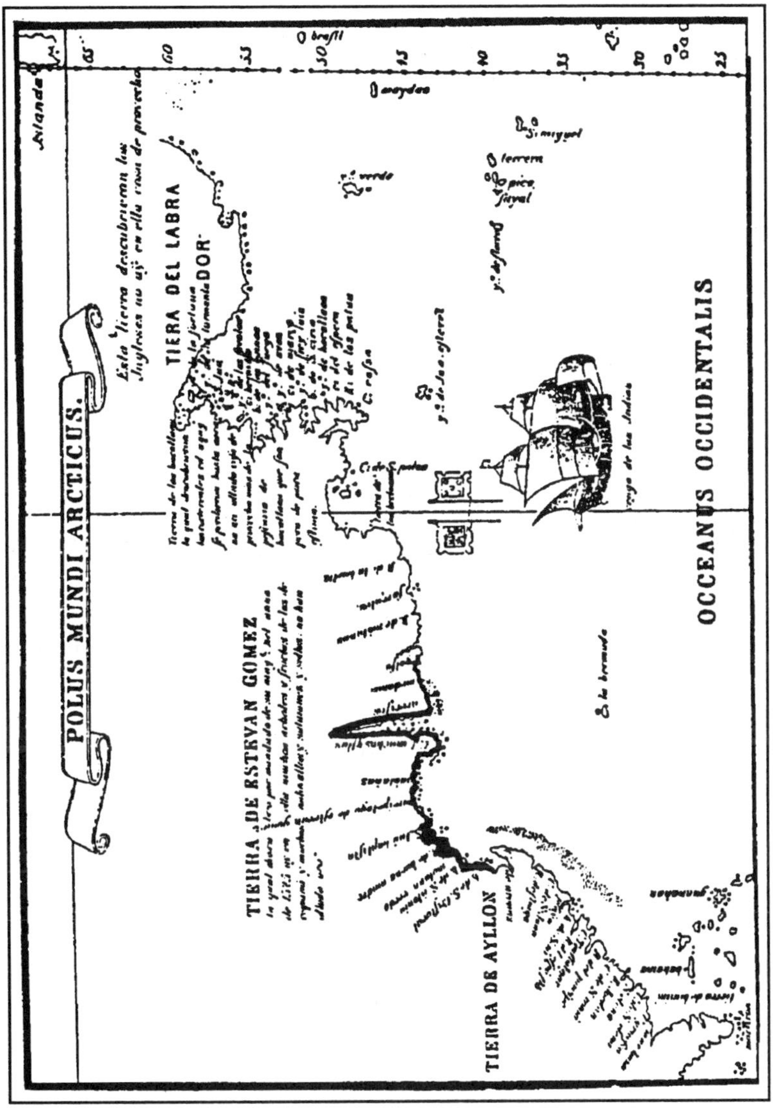

Figure 3. D. RIBERO MAP—1529

agitator was Pedro de Bazan. Gines Doncel, immediately after he saw *El Licenciado* Ayllon lying dead, saw his opportunity to seize command of the colony. Doncel held a very high opinion of himself and felt that he was the best suited for the position of governor. As always in any difficult or dangerous endeavor there are always certain faint-hearted who rather than persevere, waver in their purpose thereby becoming malcontents. The colony at San Miguel being no exception had its group of malcontents. It was to this group that Doncel appealed for support, brought a certain Pedro de Bazan to the same opinion, and together along with some other malcontents then seized the captain deputy, Francisco Gomez, and the alcalde (town council) and incarcerated them. The mutineers subsequently pursued their own selfish desires employing high-handed methods.

It was shortly after the mutiny that a group of Spaniards and their families left the settlement. Not wishing to become involved in the power struggle and internal squabbling within the colony, they sought refuge in an Indian village three leagues distant. After a time, word was received at the settlement that some (*algunos*) of them had been killed by Indians. Of the remaining Spaniards who left the settlement none reportedly returned to San Miguel, so when the colonists at San Miguel departed for Hispanola at a later date, they left behind some of their countrymen and women.

During the power struggle a small band of Indians attacked the settlement but were successfully repulsed, however, some Spaniards were killed during the attack. The killing of the Spaniards by the Indians had severe repercussions on the leadership of Doncel and Bazan. Some individuals of good sense, not being able to tolerate the tyranny and arrogance of Doncel and his followers especially after the deaths of some of their fellow colonists at the hands of the Indians, united and sought to reproach Doncel. Principal among these colonists were two hidalgos, Oliveros and Monesterio. Oliveros thus sought Doncel out and protested the imprisonment of

Captain Francisco Gomez and the alcaldes and demanded their immediate release. Doncel refused, stating that he was keeping the captain and alcaldes prisoners because Gomez and his followers planned to seize the ships and abandon the colony given their freedom.

Olivero's unsuccessful attempt in securing the release of the prisoners and his outspokenness served only to gain Doncel's enmity. His continued outspokenness against Doncel's tyranny caused Doncel and Bazan to conspire to kill the two hidalgos, Oliveros and Monesterio. On the night when they planned to put their malintention into effect, it happened that some negro slaves seeking vengeance against Doncel for his cruel treatment of them, set fire to his house. It so happened that Gines was not the sole occupant of the house as the prisoners were also being held there by him. On hearing the alarm, the entire town rushed to the fire to extinguish it, and while fighting the fire they were able to rescue the prisoners. During the confusion, Bazan saw his opportunity to put his assassination plot into effect, and he rushed to Monesterio's dwelling. Although Bazan was armed, the unarmed Monesterio managed to grab onto Bazan before the assassin could bring his weapon to use. The two men continued the struggle with hands, each one uttering curses in loud voices. In the meantime, Oliveros went searching for Doncel seeking to seize him, and as he was prowling through the streets, he heard the loud voices and tumult of the struggling combatants. He immediately ran to the scene where Monesterio was holding the knife-yielding Bazan at bay. On arriving at the scene, Oliveros thus entered the struggle and with a well-placed kick to Bazan's leg, he was able to bring Bazan to the ground where he was thus able to subdue and arrest the mutineer. Having taken Bazan as prisoner, Oliveros and Monesterio returned to the scene of the fire to resume their search of Doncel. As the fire spread out of control throughout the structure, Doncel, who all the while had been in hiding in the burning building, was forced to evacuate from his place of hiding under a couch and was immediately apprehended.

Doncel and Bazan were tried and found guilty. Bazan, who was guilty of attempted murder, was sentenced to be dragged and afterwards beheaded. Gines Doncel and some others of his confederation were tried and convicted, but of a lesser crime. After this unfortunate incident, even the staunchest of the colonists resolved to return to the Indies, and sometime during the late winter of 1527 they began their journey back to the relative comfort and safety of Hispanola. The Spaniards placed the body of Ayllon in the gabarra so as to return it either to Santo Domingo where he had his residence or Puerto de Plata where he had large land holdings and a one-half ownership in a large sugar mill. However, the exhumed body of the licenciado never reached its destination. Somewhere off the Carolina coast the gabarra foundered in an ocean tempest taking the body of Lucas Vasquez de Ayllon to the vast grave of the Ocean Sea.[14]

Oviedo relates a rare occurrence which happened during the voyage back to Santo Domingo...."The cold was so great that as they embarked, sick and malprovisioned, many died of cold. On the caravela, Santa Catalina, seven men froze to death; and on the ship Chorucca, there occurred a thing which is rare or never seen. And it happened with one of those sinners, who wishing to take off his stockings, all of the flesh of the legs stuck to the stockings around below the knees, and there remained the bare bones exposed, and that night he died.[15]

The first ship, the Breton, that departed from San Miguel de Guandape carrying some Dominicans arrived at Puerto de Plata in twenty-one days clearly waterlogged. Another ship called the Great Breton, because of its relatively large size, was not as fortunate, It was en route almost four months and it finally reached safe haven at Puerto Rico on the Island of San Juan. Of the seventy persons who sailed on it, a mere fifteen to twenty survived, the others died of hunger or thirst. Another ship ultimately landed on the island of Anegada, a small island northeast of the Virgin Islands, while another vessel reached the point of Tiburon on the southeast end of Hispanola. Finally the last ship arrived at San Fermin on the island of San Juan. On one of these ships, all of the colonists would have perished of thirst had it not been for a civilized Indian who squeezed the juice from a maguey, (century plant), filled a water bag with its liquid, and returned to the ship where the "sinners" (as Oviedo refers to the colonists) refreshed themselves.

Some of the most notable survivors, the ones who witnessed the events and subsequently reported them to Oviedo, included three members of the religious Order of Preachers (Dominicans), Fray Antonio Montesino of earlier mention and fame, Fray Antonio de Cervantes and Fray Pedro de Estrada; Francisco Gomez, the captain and deputy of the *Licenciado*; Pedro de Quexos, the head pilot; Juan Rodriguez Malaver and other trustworthy persons.

The widow of Lucas Vasquez, Dona Ana de Becerra, and his son, Lucas Vasquez Ayllon, asked that there be continuation with the agreement and the grants contained in it, since *El Licenciado* Ayllon had spent one hundred thousand ducats of his own money in the service of the King leaving his family poor. However, as in the case of Juan Ponce de Leon, the son did not prove to be of the same mettle as the father. The son of Ayllon did not immediately pursue the continuance of the agreement and no further attempt was made by an Ayllon to colonize the lands to the north of latitudes thirty-five, thirty-six and thirty-seven until the early 1560's when the younger Ayllon applied and received permission from King Felipe to settle those latitudes. Try as he might though, Ayllon the Younger was unable to raise the necessary funds and he never sailed north.

Of the five hundred colonists who went on the 1526 expedition, only one hundred fifty returned safely to the Indies. The number who remained in the interior of present-day North Carolina and Virginia is not known, however, that they survived and reproduced is a certainty. Reference to non-Indian peoples residing in the vicinity of the Albemarle/Pamlico/Chesapeake Bay area was made by other Europeans of a later date i.e. The English of Raleigh's venture (1884) and Captain John Smith of the Jamestown Colony (1607).

On the 27th day of April, 1584, Captains M. Philip Amadas and M. Arthur Barlowe set sail from the West of England in two vessels. Their goal? To reconnoiter that coast of the Atlantic Seaboard later called Virginia. The two captains sailed with full instructions from Sir Walter Raleigh to seek out the most suitable location for his proposed colony as specified in his letters patents granted by the Queens Majesty (Queen Elizabeth I). They arrived off the coast of present-day North Carolina in the vicinity of Cape Hatteras and shortly thereafter crossed the barrier island into the Pamlico/Albemarle Sound sanctuary. Captains Amadas and Barlowe probably entered into these waters through present-day Oregon inlet, although 1584 one could also cross the barrier islands immediately north of Cape Hatteras, an inlet which is no longer open.

Shortly after entering into the inner waters, Indians began to arrive in boats bringing gifts and messages of welcome. Lively exchange of goods took place between them, and as more and more Indians engaged in the trading, women and children made their appearance on the scene. Captain Barlowe, who authored the report of the journey wrote in his account describing some of the women and children. . . "Only the women wore their haire long on both sides, and the men but on one. They (women) are of colour yellowish, and their haire black for the most part, and yet we saw children that had very fine alburne, and chestnut coloured haire."[16] These physical characteristics are more descriptive of Europeans than of native American. Their principal place of residence as Barlowe relates later in his narrative was "an island," which they call Roanoke distant from the harbor by which we entered seven leagues."[17] Roanoke is distant from the place where Ayllon planted his colony at the head of Albemarle Sound a mere fifty miles. The head of the Sound is in close proximity to the village where some of the Ayllon people went to reside and remain after the other colonists retreated to the Indies. The women and children observed by Barlowe were obviously the second and third generation descendants of the Spanish at San Miguel. It should be noted the people of similar phenotype have resided since the early 1600's, forty to fifty miles north of the Spanish San Miguel in the vicinity of Suffolk, Virginia in an area of Dismal Swamp called Black Swamp. These people are oftentimes referred to as Suffolk Melungeons, and their origins are shrouded in mystery. Some of these people prefer to be called Black Dutch a label which apparently is much more socially acceptable than "Spanish" or "Melungeon." Another term frequently used by Melungeons to explain their dark complexion is "Black Irish." I have had many of them admit to me that although they knew that they were Melungeon, they claimed to be "Black Dutch," Portuguese, or Black Irish since it was preferable than being labeled Melungeon, Indian or Spanish. In recent years I have visited the area of the swamp occupied by these people and observed their physical characteristics and coloring. Their phenotypes were a perfect match for other Melungeons, Lumbees, Red Bones, Turks etc. which I observed throughout the states of Georgia, Tennessee, Virginia, the two Carolinas, northern Alabama, Louisiana, Kentucky and West Virginia.

The people which Barlowe observed and noted resided in that part of North Carolina long before any English settlers set foot on that land. It was not until the following year, 1585, that the first English colonists arrived and settled on Roanoke Island. The colony failed; its people killed off by Indians over a twenty year period.

Twenty-two years later another group of Englishmen arrived in the same vicinity, except that instead of settling in the Albemarle Sound area, they established themselves in the Bahia de Santa Maria (Chesapeake Bay) vicinity on an island in the James River near present-day Williamsburg, Virginia. Captain John Smith of the Jamestown Colony in his *True Relation, 1608*, relates that at a place called Ocanahowan there were certain men "cloathed" like him. This was later confirmed by a Powhatan Emperor who not only informed Smith of the "cloathed" people at Ocanahowan, but also of a people farther to the south of Ocanahowan where there was an abundance of "Brasse," and these people lived in walled houses.[18] The Powhatan Emperor also informed Smith that to the north beyond the Patawomacke (Potomac) some years past some people with short "coates" and "sleeves" to the "elbows" had passed that way in "shippes" like those of the English. This was probably Andre Gonzales in 1589 during his mapping and exploration of the Chesapeake Bay as far north as the Susquehanna. In recent times a coin bearing the image of King Felipe II who led Spain from 1555-1598 was found buried on the banks of the Susquehanna forty miles upstream at Columbia in southern Pennsylvania.

At a later date, Captain John Smith in his *The General Historie of Virginia* again alludes to the "cloathed" people at Ocanahowan whom he describes as five days journey from Jamestown (90 miles: five days at eighteen miles per day) where it was reported Spaniards were living. According to David Beers Quinn in his *Set Fair For Roanoke*, Ocanahowan was clearly on the Roanoke River.[19] This would place it very near Ayllon's San Miguel de Guandape and in the vicinity of where Captain Barlowe in 1584 took note of the people with yellowish coloring, fine auburn and chestnut colored hair.

According to Captain Barlowe's account of his 1584 voyage, he states that after being anchored for a few days inside the inlet, he sailed for Roanoke Island where he was well received. In talking about the other Indian Kingdoms, Barlowe mentions a particular kingdom called Sequotan (Secotan) which is a peninsula located between Albemarle Sound and Pamlico Sound. Barlowe states, "Toward the Southwest, foure dayes journey is situated a town called Sequotan, which is the southernmost town of Wingandacoa, neere unto which, sixe and twentie years past there was a ship caste away, whereof some of the people were save, and those were white people, whom the countrey people preserved. And after ten dayes remaining in an out Island uninhabited, called Wocokon (present-day Portmouth Island), they with the help of some of the dwellers of Sequotan, fastened two boates of the country together and made masses unto them, and sailes of their shirt, and having taken into them such victuals as the country yeelded, they departed after they had remained in this Island three weeks; but shortly after it seemed they were cast away, for the boates were found upon the coast, cast a land in another Island adjoining. . ."[20]

The town of Secota (Secotan) was situated on Bath Creek in upper Pamlico River according to the *John White - Thomas Harriot Map of Raleigh's Virginia, 1590.* The adjoining island on which the "white people" were castaway is probably present-day Cedar Island after which they could have made their way up the Neuse River where Francis Yeardley many years later found a large group of Spaniards residing very comfortably among a great nation called the Newxes (Neuse).[21]

Who were these castaways that the Secotans aided and later the Newxes took into their great nation? Barlowe states in 1584 that six and twenty years ago these white people were cast ashore. Six and twenty years subtracted from 1584 would place the shipwreck on the North Carolina coast sometime in the late 1550's specifically 1558. It was during that period of time that a ship bearing Pedro Menendez de Avila's son went under in rough seas somewhere off the Atlanta coastline past the Bahama Channel. Pedro Menendez de Avila then Admiral of the Ocean Fleet and later founder of San

Agustin and Santa Elena searched in vain for his son along those shores.

Consequently, we have two groups of Spaniards including women and children (Ayllon's and Menendez's) who came to those lands and remained for a time. No doubt after a time as the English began pushing north, south and west from their foothold along the James River, these people, the Melungeons, moved farther into the interior as we shall later see away from the English who came in ever greater numbers throughout the seventeenth and eighteenth centuries. Aboard English ships came indentured servants, and slaves of many nationalities from almost every country in Europe and the Middle-East which probably included some Turks.

N. Brent Kennedy in his book, *The Melungeons, The Resurrection of a Proud People*, however speculates that they might have arrived as early as the sixteenth century. Using David Beers Quinn, editor of *The Roanoke Voyages*, as his source, Kennedy states in reference to captives taken by Sir Francis Drake in his raid of the Spanish Main in 1585-86: "He (Sir Francis Drake) arrived at Roanoke Island just off the North Carolina shores, where large numbers of English soldiers implored him to take them home to England. In order to make room on his ships for the English garrison on Roanoke Island, it is believed that Drake may (and I emphasize the word may) have deposited most of these captives on the island or the nearby coast. The only record of any of these Moors reaching England is that there were apparent later negotiations to send home from England some one hundred ex-galley slaves to the 'Turkish dominions.' The Turkish dominions would certainly indicate 'Moors' or 'Muslims' and the figure of one hundred is substantially less than the total number of original captives."[22]

Although Kennedy. emphasizes "may," when it comes time to "sum-up" in his chapter, *Putting It All Together*, he states "Certainly if Drake's Moors were primarily men as we know they were, the tendency for their children to adopt the father's heritage would be (1) strong, given the patrilineal tradition of the Moors, and (2) as a result of this tendency, would better explain the widespread dissemination of the so-called 'Melungeon' heritage. Several hundred (several hundred?) Moorish men could leave a genetic and cultural heritage after but one generation, to say nothing of the estimated fourteen generations since their arrival."[23] The author does not disagree with Kennedy that one of the components of the melange (mixture) which comprises the Melungeon phenotype is Moorish and quite possibly Turkish even though Turkey ranked 29th out of 36 world populations in the gene frequency analysis of almost two hundred Melungeons tested. The author contends that the Moorish component of the present-day Melungeons arrived with the Spanish/Portuguese soldier/settlers as part of their genetic chain. The Moors having occupied the Iberian Peninsula for more than seven hundred years would certainly contribute to the Spanish/Portuguese phenotype.

But let us get back to the Moors/Turks who Kennedy contends were disembarked at Roanoke Island by Sir Francis Drake in June of 1586. Kennedy uses David Beers Quinn as his primary source for the "Turks" episode as follows: "David Beers Quinn, ed. *The Roanoke Voyages* Vol. 1, series no. 104, *The Hakluyt Society, 1952, 1953*, p. 251 and 255." On page 251, David Beers Quinn states: "He (Francis Drake) carried with him from England parts of boats and small ships, shoes and clothing and other equipment for the Isthmus venture. At Santo Domingo and Cartagena he had also been collecting men-galley slaves (mainly Moors, but including some Europeans), a few soldiers (again mainly Moors), negro domestic slaves to whom he promised their freedom, and a substantial number of South American Indians (about 300) including women, all of whom being acclimatized, he reckoned would help him to cross the Isthmus. Whether these motley passengers were responsible for the outbreaks of sickness among his own men we cannot say, nor can we tell how many of them succumbed, but he had not set any of them on shore when he turned back from Cartagena, decided not to attempt Havana, and made for Florida and Virginia. By that time it was clear that he planned to leave all of them except the Moors and European galley slaves at the Virginia settlement."

On pages 254 and 255, Quinn states: "The mystery of Drake's dealing with the Roanoke settlement lies in question what did he do with his passengers? He had perhaps 300 South American Indians and 100 negro slaves to dispose of as a free labour for the Roanoke settlers. Were some of them lost in the storm? Were they all set on shore, with the pots and pans of San Agustin, to make what sort of life they could for themselves? If so, did Raleigh's ship and Grenville's expedition find any trace of them? If not, did they die or were they killed on the way to England, or were they landed at Portsmouth? The only trace we find of the passengers is of negotiations to send home some 100 galley slaves to the Turkish dominions, which was probably done."[24] Quinn is very clear on the disposition of the Moors. He does not suggest that they were left behind at Roanoke. The suggestion that anyone was left behind at Roanoke was posed as a rhetorical question not as a statement of fact. Quinn wrote about this subject again in 1983 when his article, *Turks Moors Blacks and Others in Drake's West Indian Voyage* appeared in Terrae Incognitae. At that time he was even more emphatic that no Moors or Turks had been deposited by Drake at Roanoke Island as he writes: "Perhaps then, we may assume that, from an early stage in his raiding, and certainly once the Chagres venture had been given up, Drake intended that the rescued individuals (apart from the Turkish and Moorish galley slaves who had been promised freedom and repatriation) should reinforce the Roanoke colony, providing it, for instance with free black settlers."[25]

As it turned out the Roanoke colony was not in need of reinforcements since Governor Ralph Lane decided to board Drake's ships and return to England, but not before a powerful storm hit the Atlantic Seaboard sinking many of Drake's smaller ships and probably taking most of the negroes and South American Indians with them to the bottom of the sea. The fate of the Turks, however is not a mystery. Included in the 200 or so galley slaves were Turks, Frenchmen and Greeks. Of these two hundred, one hundred were ascertained to be Turks as Quinn writes in 1983: "The galley slaves ascertained to be 'Turk' — that is, subjects of the sultan were another story. As early as August 4, 1586, the Privy Council wrote to the Levant Company to ask them to consider how the 100 Turks brought by Sir Francis Drake out of the West Indies may upon the arrivall of the shipes to Wolwich and Blackwell be receyved by order of their Companie and enlarged untill they shall sende some of their shipes into those partes, in which they maye be conveyed home and presented by the Ambassador unto the Grand Seignour."[26] The other one hundred galley slaves of other nationalities who survived the voyage from Cartagena to England probably went home to their native lands as there is no evidence that anyone was left behind at Roanoke Island. In fact, ten Frenchmen were brought back to Morlaix.

In 1985, Quinn again wrote about Drake's 1585-86 West Indian venture in his book, *Set Fair For Roanoke*. Quinn is very brief on the subject of the disposition of the galley slaves and blacks as he writes: ...."What was to happen to the equipment and men intended to reinforce the colony was never indicated. His blacks and his released prisoners would presumably have to go to England."[27] On June 18,1586, Drake departed for England taking everyone with him. But how can we be so certain that he took all the surviving non-English passengers with him including the former galley slaves? According to Richard Hakluyt, author of *Hakluyt's Voyages, The Principal Navigations Voyages Traffiques and*

Discoveries of the Enalish Nation, Anno Dom. 1600, Drake departed from Plymouth, England on September 12, 1585 with "five and twenty sails of ships and pinnasses, and having assembled of souldiers and marines, to the number of 2300 in the whole." Hakluyt makes no mention whatever of Moors, Turks, South American Indians or Negroes being left behind at Roanoke, for he mentions them none at all. Hakluyt, however provides us with a clue as to why Drake would have been very foolish to have left behind experienced seamen such as the galley slaves, i.e. Turks, Moors, Greeks, Frenchmen. Quite simply, he needed them to sail his ships. Hakluyt informs us that during the voyage, Drake lost some seven hundred and fifty men (almost one third of his complement), about three fourths of them to sickness before he departed from Cartagena on the South American Continent.[28] It is no wonder then that he abandoned the Isthmus venture, bypassed powerfully fortified Havana, and did not want to risk the remainder of his men to the shoals at Santa Elena. In essence, Drake had more ships than men to sail and man them. Why would he leave behind seafaring men? He had more than ample room and supplies for the Roanoke colony aboard his larger ships. As for the South American Indians, some of them escaped along the voyage from Cartagena to San Agustin during the frequent wood-and-water stops. Ironically it was an escaped (or released) Spanish prisoner who provided Spanish officials in Cuba with the information concerning the 300 South American Indians (mostly women) and 200 negroes, Turks, and Moors reputed to have been aboard Drake's ships.

Quinn states in 1983 (Terrae Incognita), that there is no confirmation to the above report about the removal of Indians from Cartagena, and that the removal of the Indians may have been only rumor, although the statement sounded as if it were better founded.[29] Quinn adds: "If Drake did take Indians, one possibility is that he merely put them ashore again further up the coast." The present author reviewed the ships' logs of all the principal vessels in Drake's fleet, and was unable to find any mention of anyone being left behind at Roanoke. In addition, a review was made of the account of the ship sent in the year 1586 to provide relief to Lane's colony at Roanoke. The ship arrived at Roanoke on the 22nd of June 1586, four days after Drake departed for England with Lane and his people. The captain and crew of the ship returned to England after being unable to find anyone in the vicinity of Roanoke. In addition about two weeks later, early in July of 1586, three more English ships under the command of Sir Richard Grenville also arrived at Roanoke. Grenville conducted a more thorough search than the lone vessel had previously performed. He, too, was unable to find anyone in the vicinity of Roanoke or down coast. Grenville, however left fifteen men behind to retain possession of the country.

N. Brent Kennedy in his book, *The Melungeons*, in spite of the above information being available to him, states: "It does seem plausible, if not likely that these Moors and Indians were indeed put ashore at Roanoke, and that they probably made good use of the provisions left behind by the vacating English. The provisions undoubtedly included small boats for ferrying to and from the mainland. By virtue of the records, it is a given (fact) that the majority were not taken back to England, and again, it is inconceivable that Drake would have murdered them. Only weeks later (days later), an expedition to Roanoke Island by Sir Walter Raleigh reported finding no one on the island. Given the desperate circumstances of these people, it makes exceedingly good sense that they would have abandoned the island as quickly as feasible. Why would they wait for either the English or, worse still, pursuing Spanish or Portuguese ships to come recapture them? I agree with Robert Gilmer that if the three-hundred-plus unaccounted-for captives were indeed left behind at Roanoke, they would have vacated the island at the earliest opportunity."[30] (Robert Gilmer is an Abingdon, Virginia physician).

The author does not totally discount the Turkish component of the Melungeon equation, however, the author very emphatically disagrees that the Turkish input was provided as early as the sixteenth century, i.e. by way of the Drake/Roanoke episode. The Turkish input probably was not provided until late in the seventeenth century; by that time the Melungeons, descendants of the Pardo people, had already been in the interior of the Southeastern United States for more than one hundred years.

PART 2
THE HISTORY—JUAN PARDO

Captain Juan Pardo was part of a large contingent of soldier/settlers who sailed from San Lucar, Spain in the Spring of 1566 under the command of Sancho de Aciniega. The fleet consisted of seventeen ships, fifteen hundred men, fourteen Spanish women, and an abundant supply of armament, munitions, and provisions.[1] Most of the men and women were recruited by Pedro Menendez de Avila, Governor and Captain-General of La Florida, in Galicia, Northern Portugal and the Asturias, Menendez's own homeland. Although the fleet departed from Spain during the Easter season of 1566, it was not until late June of that same year when they finally arrived at San Agustin. Upon arriving at San Agustin, Aciniega was informed that the fledgling colony at Santa Elena further up the coast was in dire need of men and supplies.

Shortly thereafter, de Aciniega dispatched Captain Pardo and two hundred fifty men northward to succor the beleaguered settlement. Pardo carried special orders from Aciniega which would have divided the command at Fort San Felipe between Pardo and Estevan de Las Alas who was at that time already at Santa Elena. Las Alas took exception with the orders and refused to comply with Aciniega's wishes. Rather than force a showdown with Las Alas, Pardo agreed to forego the special orders and abided with Las Alas's argument that only he (Las Alas) could command at Fort San Felipe. Consequently, Pardo elected not to reside inside the fort, so he and his men commenced to build quarters for themselves outside of the fort. Pardo's camp and quarters were situated on the north side of the fort and were the beginnings of the town of Santa Elena which would, at a later date, become known as Beaufort, South Carolina. Pardo's camp would eventually house the first Spanish families who would soon arrive prepared to make a new life for themselves in the Carolina wilderness.

Pedro Menendez de Avila himself with the help of the cacique Orista (Edisto) selected the site of the Spanish fort. During the fourth week of April, 1566, Menendez, in company with Orista, examined the site of the proposed Spanish town and fort. Both Menendez and Orista, in whose territory the fort and town would lie, agreed that it was a very pleasant location. The location of the site was approximately one and one-half leagues south of the village of Orista (The French called it Stalame. See LeMoyne map 1591) and about three fourths league upstream on the present-day Beaufort River from Chowan Spit.[2] Ribaut and the French had built a very crude and short-lived fort in 1562 in the same general present day locality (See LeMoyne map 1591). On the very day that the site was selected, Menendez, De Las Alas, and the other captains marked out the fort. Its construction was entrusted to Antonio Gomez, whom the Adelantado Menendez had personally selected for the task. To Gomez were assigned fifty Spanish soldiers and some seamen from the ship-of-fleet. Their task was to construct a strong defensible presidio in the shortest time possible. The stockade was constructed of stakes, earth and fascines; and six bronze field pieces were located strategically within the enclosure. The Adelantado named the fort for His Majesty, Don Felipe. Fort San Felipe was situated almost at the extreme southeast tip of present-day Port Royal Island atop a white barranca (ravine) where today is located the deep water port of Port Royal, South Carolina just south of the city of Beaufort.[3] At a later date in 1578, the fort was relocated two hundred paces further up the peninsula toward

Beaufort, and it was renamed Fort San Marcos. The town of Santa Elena lay north of the new fort and south and slightly west of present-day Spanish Point in south Beaufort. San Marcos lay between the town of Santa Elena and the harbor looking downstream on the Beaufort River toward the harbor entrance. The distance from the fort to the forest on the north was two hundred fifty paces.

During the founding of Fort San Felipe in April of 1566, Menendez was visited by local caciques, including Orista, imploring him to send to them Christians to live among them and to teach them the Holy Gospel. During the fifteen days that the Adelantado remained at San Felipe many other Indian caciques from the interior came to Santa Elena to meet with him and to ask for Christians to go live with them and instruct them in Christian doctrine. Menendez complied with their requests, giving each cacique one or two Christians and tools with which to construct a cross in each Indian town. To each cacique he also gave presents and a hatchet which delighted the caciques and as they departed to return to their own villages, they pledged their loyalty. Menendez departed from Santa Elena during the first week of May, 1566, leaving De Las Alas in command.

When Menendez returned to Santa Elena in August of 1566, he found Juan Pardo constructing dwellings outside of the fort for his men. The Adelantado had other plans for Pardo. The long-awaited road to New Spain must be completed. Tristan de Luna in 1559 had opened the road from Santa Maria de Ichuse (present-day Pensacola, Florida) to Chiaha in northwestern present-day Georgia. Pardo's task was to open the road from Santa Elena to Chiaha thereby completing an overland route from the Gulf of Mexico to the Atlantic Ocean, and so offering an alternate route to the treacherous sea route via the Bahama Channel.

The journey of Captain Juan Pardo into the interior of what is today South Carolina, Georgia, Tennessee, Alabama and North

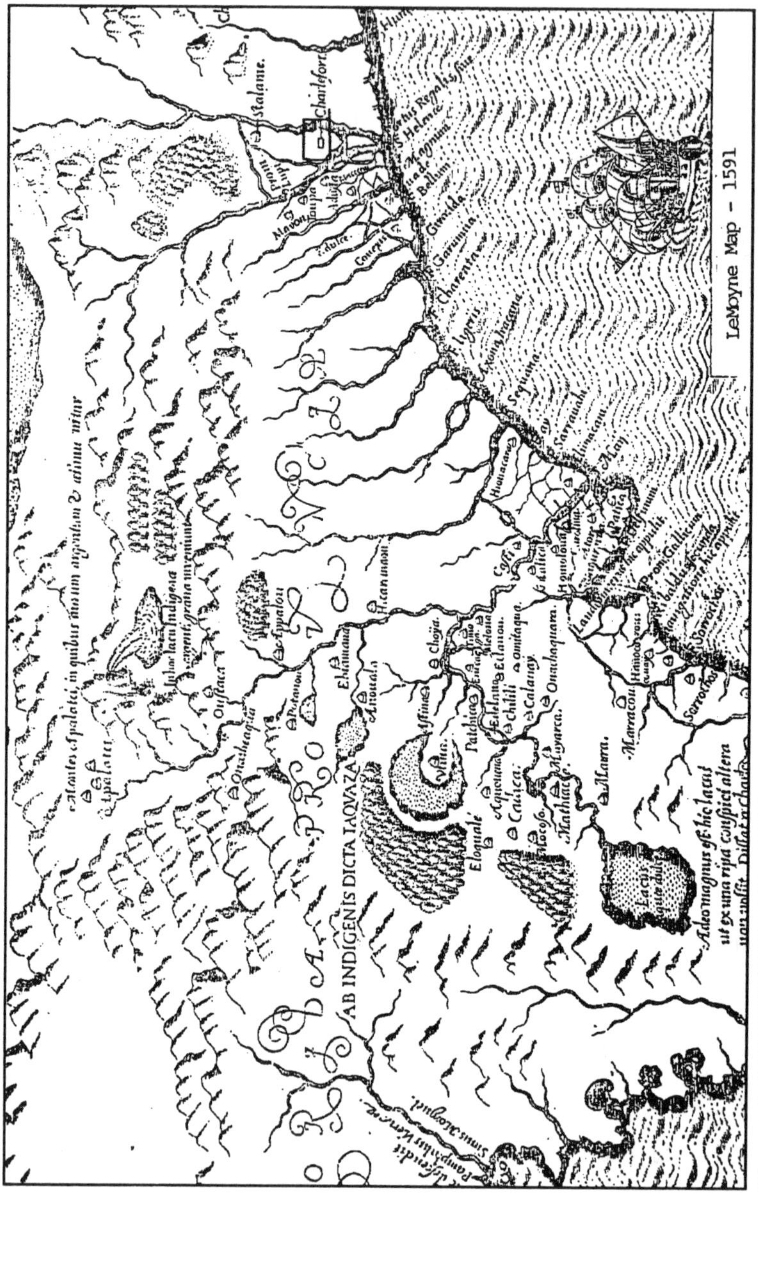

Figure 4. LEMOYNE MAP—1591

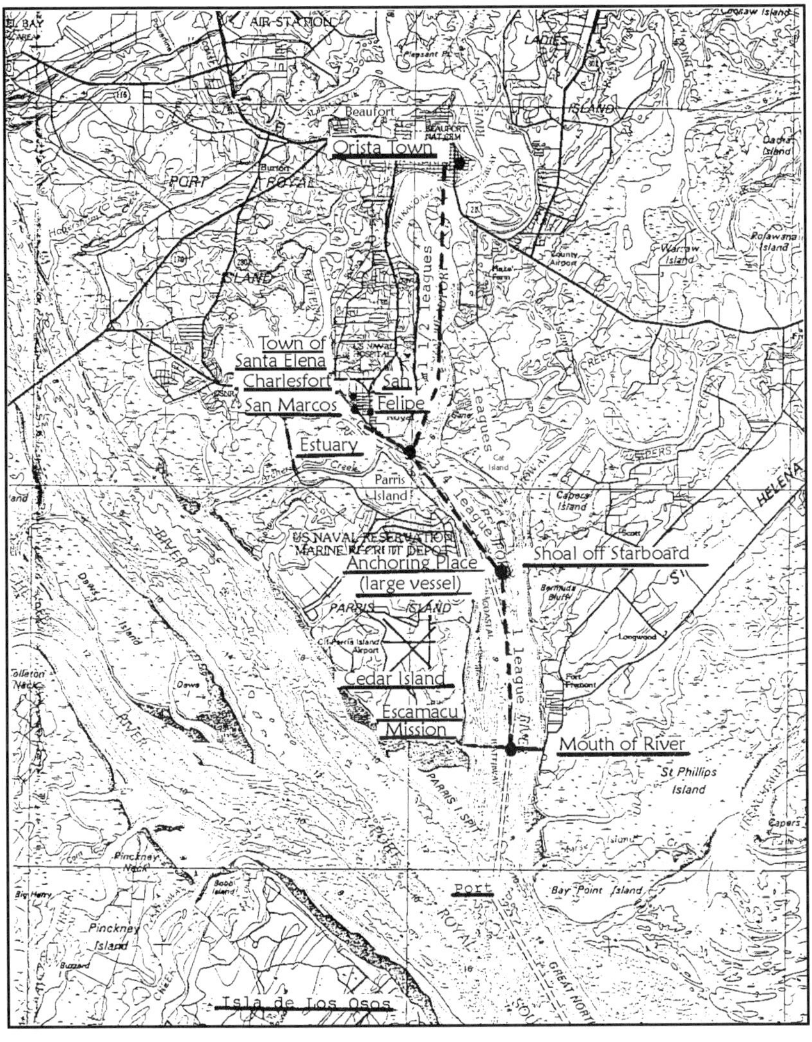

Figure 5. SANTA ELENA

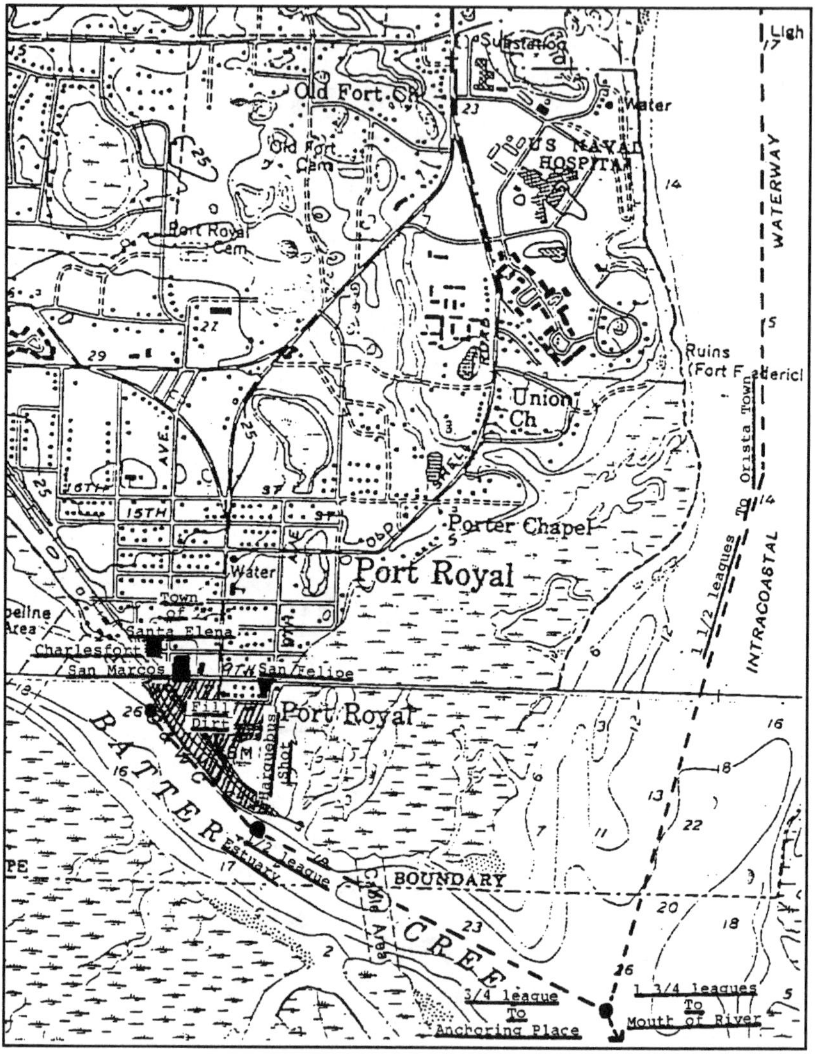

Figure 6. SANTA ELENA

Figure 7. PORT ROYAL ISLAND—SANTA ELENA

Figure 8. PORT ROYAL ISLAND—SANTA ELENA

Carolina is noteworthy in that his path-of-travel took him along Indian trails which today are major highways. Those trails led to Indian villages which today are modern, thriving towns. Pardo and his men built no less than four forts and two settlement towns in the interior; and as late as the later part of the sixteenth century, those Spaniards, Pardo's men and their families were still living in the general area where their captain stationed them—more than three hundred miles in the interior of the present-day Southeastern United States. The area that his journeys covered was extensive, and the permanent knowledge gained by Pardo and his followers concerning the land and its people contributed significantly to the ultimate settlement of those areas by other Europeans. It is interesting to note that his path crossed and re-crossed the paths of De Soto and of Don Tristan de Luna Y Arellano, and that the Indians, who dealt with his two predecessors when they traversed that self-same land, for the most part, were favorably disposed toward Pardo and his Spaniards and often accepted them as friends and asked for Christians to remain and teach them the Holy Gospel. Those Indians were, for the most part, the same Indians whom historians have repeatedly accused De Soto and his men of abusing and heaping degradation upon degradation. Strange that they should then welcome Pardo and his few soldiers so openly. It is fortunate for the telling of the historical account, as was the custom of the Spanish of that time, that not one, but two, and often three individuals recorded the events of such an enterprise. Pardo's two journeys into the interior were recorded by Pardo himself, and by one of the men who accompanied him, the notary Juan de La Vandera. Another man, a soldier, one Francisco Martinez, gives the account of the activities of Sergeant Bayano whom Pardo stationed along with thirty men in 1566 at San Juan de Juada near present day Helen in northeast Georgia.

Menendez allowed Pardo one hundred fifty men for the venture into the interior, and ordered him to depart from Santa Elena on St.

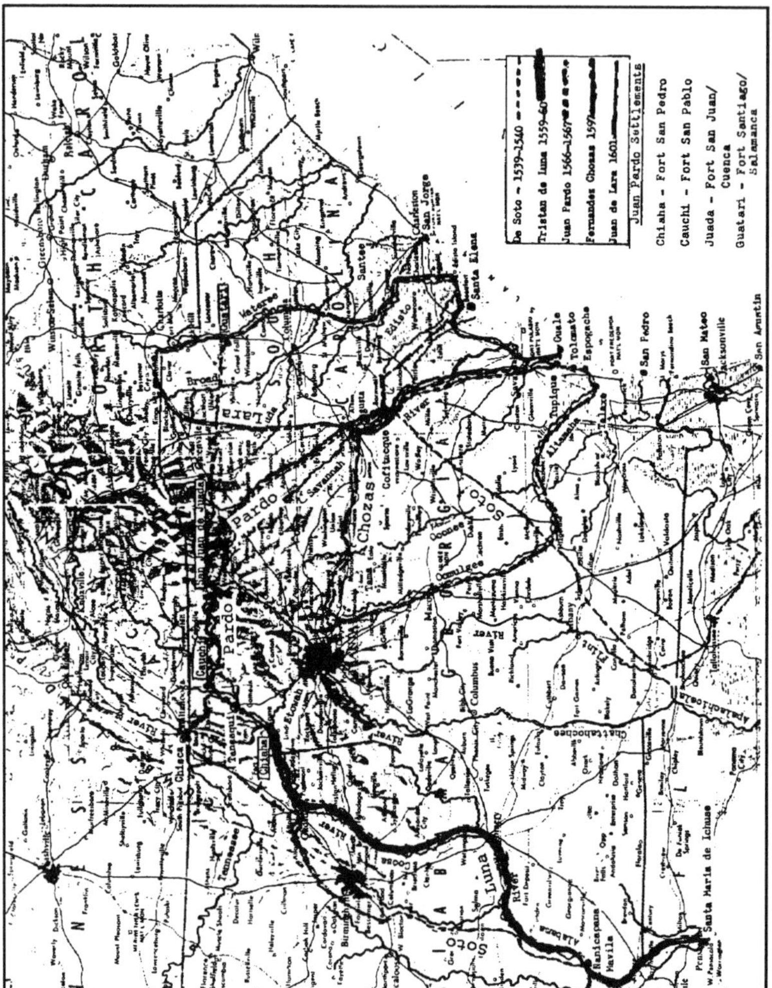

Figure 9. JUAN PARDO SETTLEMENTS

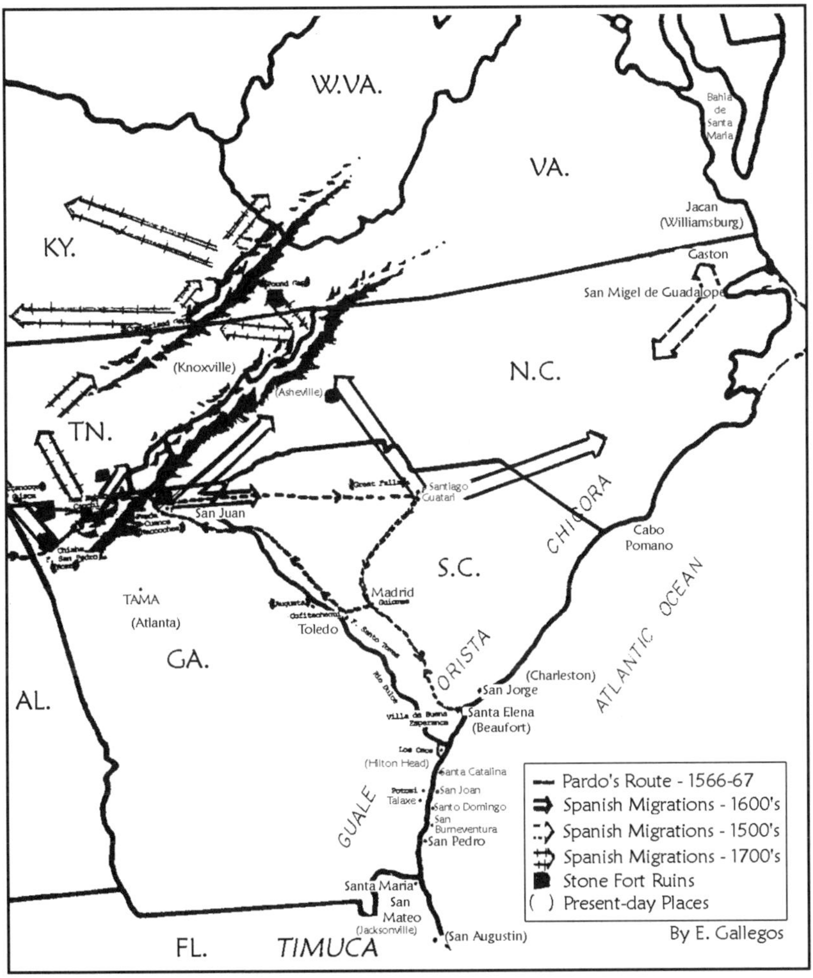

Figure 9. SPANISH MIGRATIONS

Andrew's Feast Day, December 1, 1566.[4] On the day of his departure, however, Pardo departed with only one hundred twenty-five men. His first night camp was at the Indian village of Escamacu fifteen miles northwest of Santa Elena on an island near present-day Seabrook, South Carolina. This was probably the same populus Indian village that Jean Rebaut visited on his brief overnight stay with the Escamacu Indians. Pardo gave the first of many speeches or harangues pertaining to the greatness of His Most Holiness, the Pope, and Don Felipe, His Majesty King of Spain, and to the need for the Indians to come under both of their services and protection. The Indians received and responded positively to the harangues.

From Escamacu, Pardo went directly to Ahoya another island town located at the mouth of the Coosawhatchie River just as it enters the Broad River from the northwest. As at Escamacu, he found the land good and well suited for maize. From Ahoya his line-of-travel took him up the Coosawhatchie, however, he did not necessarily follow the river bank because of the swamps and marches along its banks. Instead, he followed the higher land between the Coosawhatchie on the west and the Combahee on the east until the Combahee becomes the Salkehatchie a few miles north of Jonesville, South Carolina. He came across several small Indian communities along the course of travel, and in all those towns, he was well received. Again, it was noted by Vandera that the land was rich and capable of producing numerous types of grains, grapes and other species of fruit like those of Spain. By the fifth day of travel, Pardo and his men had reached the fall-line and above, and as their course took them closer to the Salkehatchie River, they arrived at the Indian town of Guiomaer, which was located near present-day Barnwell, South Carolina. Both Pardo and Vandera agree that Guiomaer was about forty leagues from the Punta de Santa Elena and could be reached by following the river downstream.[5] At Guiomaer, he gave the usual harangue before proceeding to the next town about ten leagues to the northwest which he reached in two days. The town was the largest yet that he had visited. It was called by two names, Cano or Cofitacque, and was on a very large river which at a later date became known as the Savannah River.[6]

By direct line, Cofitacque is thirteen miles below Augusta, Georgia at Siver Bluff on the South Carolina side of the state line. Silver Bluff is less than five miles from Jackson, South Carolina. According to both of the writers, Pardo and Vandera, it was serviced by several good-sized fresh water streams, and the reddish dirt was excellent for growing a large variety of grain, vegetables, and fruits. Vandera tells us that its ideal location gave it the capability of becoming an even larger town. It was fifty leagues from Santa Elena, and it could be reached both by traveling overland or by following the river to the sea then proceeding north toward the Punta de Santa Elena. Cofitacque is the same Cofitacque of De Soto's time. It was this same Indian town that was ruled by the "Lady of Cofitacque" who befriended De Soto and his men. From Cofitacque, Pardo proceeded up the Carolina side of the Savannah River as far as present-day Augusta, Georgia to the Indian village of Tagaya where he had the caciques and Indians brought together and received their pledge to render service to the Pope and to the King. At every town and village that he visited, he received the Indians' pledge of faithful service. As he traveled through the South Carolina wilderness, Pardo took note and recorded his observations pertaining to the land, trees, crops and disposition of the Indians. In this manner he proceeded in a northwesterly direction through several minor Indian villages of Tagaya, Chiquito, Gueza, Ysa and finally to the much larger Indian town of Xuada or Juada in the mountains of northeast Georgia. Pardo's line-of-travel probably took him past Toccoa, Georgia after he left the country around the Savannah River. Juada was the same Juada of De Soto and was situated in the vicinity of Nacoochee,

Georgia and probably not too far distant from Helen and Sautee, Georgia on the upper reaches of the Chattachoochee just inside the territory occupied by the Cherokee Indians. Prior to this time, Pardo and his men had been traveling within the territory of the Creek Indians in the interior of Georgia and South Carolina and the Cusabo Indians closer to the coast of South Carolina.

Juada appears to have been the first major stopping-off place for Pardo. He and his men remained at Juada for fifteen days resting and reconnoitering the countryside. At the end of fifteen days, he proceeded north along the Chattachoochee River, but not before constructing a fort and detailing his Sergeant Bayano to remain behind with thirty soldiers with orders to defend the fort and hold the land for the King. Juan de La Vandera, one of the soldier/chroniclers noted that the land of Juada was beautiful much like that of the majority of Spain, good for all kinds of species of things which men desire to cultivate. Francisco Martinez, one of Pardo's men who was assigned to Fort San Juan at Juada under Sergeant Bayano, gives a more vivid and detailed account of the country abounding with game, such as deer, hare, rabbits, chickens, bears and lions. Vandera is the only one of the three chroniclers (Martinez, Pardo and Vandera) who gives an approximate distance from Juada to the Punta de Santa Elena which he states is about one hundred leagues or about two hundred seventy miles on the march.[7] After departing from Juada, Pardo followed an ancient Indian trail later known as the Unicoi Trail. He spent one night in camp in the direction of the north. Due to the lateness of the season which was well into December, he encountered snow in the mountains. At this point, he was within ten miles of Brasstown Bald Mountain, the highest mountain in the vicinity of Fort San Juan. Brasstown Bald rises almost five thousand feet elevation above sea level. The following day Pardo turned back along the Chattahoochee, but did not pass through Juada. Instead, he turned toward the left and followed another ancient trail, later known as the Tugaloo Trail

Figure 11. SAN JUAN DE JUADA—Located in present-day Georgia north of Atlanta. San Juan was Juan Pardo's main post during his settlement of the interior in 1566-67. In addition to the fort, the Spanish also established the town-settlement of Cuenca. The ruins of the Spanish fort are still visible atop Alec Mountain in the Helen, Georgia, vicinity.

which ran in an east-west direction toward present-day South Carolina.[8] After camping out two nights in uninhabited areas, he arrived at the Indian town of Quinahaqui which was on a large river, probably the Saluda River in the vicinity of present-day Greenville, South Carolina. The area around Quinahaqui was very pleasant with many beautiful green places and lush meadows. Pardo remained here four days. After leaving Quinahaqui, Pardo continued along the same line-of-travel, and after one day's travel arrived at another Indian village with lush green meadows. The name of the town was Guatariatique, and like the many other Indian towns that Pardo and his men had visited and would visit, it, too, was situated on a large river which in this case was probably the Tyger River about ten miles southwest of present-day Union, South Carolina. Here, also, as he had done in the numerous other Indian towns, Pardo and his men were well received by the Indians. Pardo obtained their pledge to honor and obey the Pope and His Majesty as the first step in becoming Christians. After a two day stopover at Guatariatique, Pardo proceeded to Guatari which was fifteen to sixteen leagues to the east and a shade to the south of the prior town. Pardo's line-of-march took him across the Broad River fifteen miles east of the Tyger. He arrived at Guatari during the second day of travel. Guatari, according to the chroniclers, was on a large river which almost certainly is the present-day Catawba/Wateree River as it rolls through the green hills of South Carolina not far from the old Indian townsite of Mulberry and Adamson dating back to A.D. 1000. Pardo at this point was in the heart of Catawba lands. Vandera describes the setting as hilly with very rich lands and having very good houses and huts and round terraces. He adds that the land is arable and capable of growing all plants known to Spaniards. The distance from Guatari to Santa Elena according to Vandera it is eighty leagues or about two hundred ten miles, and the first twenty leagues of this river system

Figure 12. WALKING THROUGH THE CAROLINA WOODS–
Most of the Spanish movement into the interior of the southeastern regions of the interior of the Southeastern United States was by foot. Except for a few instances during which horses were used. The Spanish had to not only travel by foot but also carry their luggage. The dense foliage of the interior country and the swamps along the coast made travel by horse impractical. The horses which were used were usually a smaller variety of animal called "sumpter" horses or mules. These animals could work their way with greater ease through the thick forests, than could horses of a larger variety.

can be navigated by any size ship.[9] The river system referred to above is the Wateree-Santee River system of South Carolina.

Pardo reports that on arriving at Guatari, he and his men were greeted by more than thirty caciques and a large number of Indians, some of whom were women and who held an equal status with the men. Vandera adds that the female caciques were served by pages and women. Pardo made the usual harangue to the caciques and Indians, and as a result, the caciques asked him to leave someone with them to teach them the faith. The Spaniards had been at Guatari fifteen or sixteen days when a letter from Estevan de Las Alas arrived with orders for Pardo to return to Santa Elena since the threat of French intrusion in the King's La Florida and Santa Elena provinces appeared imminent. Pardo departed from Guatari immediately, however, he honored the caciques' requests and assigned a knowledgeable person to remain behind to instruct the Indians. Also, he assigned some soldiers to remain behind to protect the instructor, and also to raise a fort for the King's service. Pardo returned to Santa Elena, however, the French intrusion did not materialize, and Pardo remained at Santa Elena awaiting further orders.

In the meantime, while Pardo was waiting at Santa Elena for the French to arrive, Sergeant Bayano and fifteen soldiers engaged a large force of Indians in a neighboring province toward and north in combat. Pardo had not been back at Santa Elena very long when he received a communication from Bayano informing him that he had engaged a cacique named Chisca, who was a longtime enemy of the Spaniards, in war and that during the battle, they the Spaniards, had slain more than one thousand Indians and burned fifty huts and that his men had suffered little injury with only two being wounded, and none seriously. In the same letter Bayano asked for instructions as how he should proceed, i.e. should he remain in Fort San Juan at Juada, or should he venture forth to the lands toward the west and New Spain?

While Bayano's letter and Pardo's subsequent reply were in transit, a cacique from Chisca arrived at Fort San Juan to intimidate Bayano and his men at Juada. The Chisca warrior informed the Spaniards that a force of Indians large enough to meet and deal, and defeat them was en route. Bayano apparently was not a man to be intimidated easily, and rather than sit in the relative safety of Fort San Juan and await the arrival of the enemy, he and twenty soldiers set out for Chisca which was on a very large river.[10] Chisca was a Yuchi town in present-day Tennessee in the vicinity of Chattanooga. The large river close to Chisca was the Tennessee River of the present day. This Yuchi town was the Chisca of De Soto's day and not Chiaha as is popularly believed. The De Soto Quad Centennial Commission established by Congress in 1938 to determine De Soto's route, erroneously called the Yuchi town, Chiaha, placing Chiaha at or below Chattanooga, when in actuality Chiaha was in the vicinity of present-day Rome, Georgia at the junction of the Etowah and Oostanaula Rivers. The two rivers come together at Rome to form the Coosa River. While at Chiaha, De Soto dispatched a squad of soldiers to Chisca, an Indian town to the north of Chiaha, to a place where the mountains rose sharply from the surrounding hills. The Congressional Commission concluded that that squad of men probably reached the Cumberland Plateau in the vicinity of Crab Orchard, Tennessee. The high mountains referred to, which rise sharply out of the surrounding hills, are the high ridges of Lookout Mountain and East Ridge in the Chattanooga area and not the Cumberland Plateau.

Bayano arrived at Chisca in the early morning hours, and as he approached the Yuchi Indian stronghold, he noticed that the greatest concentration of warriors was located in a high, fortified' stockaded tower with only one entrance, a very small door. Bayano quickly analyzed the situation and determined that the only way to capture the town was to take the tower. He and his men made a foray at the tower using their shields for cover with Bayano at the point, and his men fanning out at uniform intervals behind him. With great risk to them, the Spaniards were successful in gaining the tower. The Indians who had been fortified in the tower, on realizing that the tower was lost, retreated from the wooden fortress and regrouped in their underground ceremonial chambers, and subsequently they emerged to engage the Spaniards in an open field of combat. The charge by the Chiscas failed, and according to Martinez, the soldier/chronicler, more than two thousand Indians perished by fire since, as they retreated into their huts or houses, the Spaniards set fire to the houses with the occupants still in them.

After the battle, the Spaniards remained at Chisca for a short time, and it was there the letter from Captain Pardo, who was still at Santa Elena, arrived ordering Bayano to leave ten men to hold the fort at Juada and continue with the remaining twenty soldiers in the direction of New Spain. Thus, Bayano took to the march again, and after traveling four days, he arrived at Chiaha, which as noted previously, was located in the vicinity of present-day Rome, Georgia at the confluence of the Etowah and the Oostanaula Rivers and not too far distant from the Indian mound ruins at Etowah, Georgia. The mounds at Etowah are one of the largest remnants of an ancient Indian peoples. At Chiaha the Spaniards encountered an enclosed town with two wooden towers similar to the tower at Chisca. Martinez informs us that the town was stockaded between two rivers with much water and that in the town, there were more than three thousand Indians, there being no women and children present. The women and children had been taken to a hiding place much in the manner that they had been hidden when Arellano's Spaniards had approached this very town a few years earlier in 1559. Bayano and his men, unlike the reception at Chisca, were well-received at Chiaha and fed by the Indians. It should be recalled at this time that the Indians at Chiaha had in the past been on friendly terms with the Spaniards. It was at Chiaha that Tristan de Luna y Arellano's men had been so openly welcomed by the natives in 1559 when De Luna's men spent several months waiting for instructions from Tristan at Pensacola to proceed ahead and open the road to Santa Elena. The Spaniards of that day (1559) knew Chiaha as the principal town of the Coosa Indians. Unfortunately, Tristan de Luna's men advanced no further east than Chiaha at Rome, Georgia. However, during a period of less than ten years (1559-1567) the entire distance from Santa Maria de Ichuse (Pensacola Bay, Florida) to Santa Elena (Port Royal, South Carolina) had been traversed and mapped by men of Spain.

After overnighting at Chiaha, Bayano turned west and followed a parallel course along the Coosa River as it flowed its first few miles through western Georgia then crossed the rugged Lookout Mountains in northeastern Alabama. One of the soldier/chroniclers describes this area as even more rugged than the ones west of Juada. The small Spanish force traveled southwest for twelve days before arriving at a large Coosa Indian town located north and east of Tuscaloosa, Alabama. Here, as at Chiaha, the Spaniards were well-received, and the cacique offered some of his warriors to the Spaniards to aid them in constructing a fort. The Spaniards elected not to build the fort, did not remain long at Coosa, and soon headed back to Chiaha. Pardo, in the meantime, returned to the interior in September, 1567, while Bayano and his men were at Chiaha.

While Bayano was engaged with the King's affairs in the wilderness of interior Georgia and Alabama, Captain Pardo remained at Santa Elena awaiting either the French or Pedro Menendez. Menendez was first to arrive at Santa Elena, and with him he brought word that the French invasion was not going to materialize. Subsequently, he ordered Pardo back into the interior to resume his search for a road to New Spain. Pardo and his contingent left Santa Elena on September 1, 1567. He carried with him special instructions from the Adelantado concerning the objectives of the second entry.[11] The first order was to open a road to New Spain; the second, to make friends and allies with all the Indians along the way; and third, to give them clerics to teach them the Holy Christian religion. Juan de La Vandera, royal notary, accompanying Pardo, was instructed by Menendez to remind the Captain (Pardo) that he inquire of the caciques if they desired to be Christians and give obedience to the Pope and to His Majesty. If they so desired, clerics would be sent to them to teach them Christianity. If the caciques did not give possession of their land to His Majesty, it would be taken and held in his name.

Pardo was instructed by Menendez to make friends with all the caciques, and to attempt to persuade them to give obedience to His Majesty. The Adlantado further instructed Pardo that wherever he arrived at a principal town, he was to leave a cross and a Christian who would teach them the Christian doctrine. Menendez admonished Pardo that he was to insure that the persons who remained behind at the Indian towns conduct themselves in an honorable and disciplined manner. The Adelantado allowed one hundred twenty soldiers, harquebusiers, and crossbowmen to execute the opening of a road to New Spain.[12] Pardo also took with him Guillermo Rufin as interpreter. Rufin was a Frenchman who had come with Ribaut a few years earlier when the French had established a short-lived fort (Charlesfort) near Fort San Felipe on Port Royal Island. Rufin had remained at Charlesfort rather than risk the Atlantic crossing, since shortly after Ribaut departed from Charlesfort, the men mutinied, killed their commander, Albert, and departed for France. Rufin subsequently fell into Spanish hands shortly after the Spanish under Rojas arrived seeking the French.

Pardo departed on September 1, 1567, on his second entry into the interior. Essentially, he followed the same route as before as far as the river crossing north of present-day Augusta, Georgia. Instead of crossing the river to the Georgia side as he had done in 1566, he remained on the South Carolina side of the Savannah River and followed the highland ridge on the right bank of the river. His line-of-march was probably along present-day South Carolina State Road 31 to Anderson, South Carolina, and then to present-day Greenville, South Carolina in the vicinity of the Indian town of Quinahaqui. At Quinahaqui he turned west and by-passed the Indian town of Ysa or present-day Toccoa, Georgia, which lay to the left of his line-of-march. Vandera notes that the area around Ysa had very beautiful meadows, many rivers, springs and three crystal mines which Pardo registered in case it should come to pass one day that they might desire to mine them.

On the third day after departing from Quinahaqui, he arrived at Juada only to discover that his Sergeant Bayano was not at Fort San Juan. The ten men whom Bayano had left at the fort were under seige by the Indians. These men were holed-up behind the fort walls patiently waiting for reinforcements to arrive to lift the siege. Pardo quickly dispersed the Indians, and he ordered them to gather in front of the fort where he wished to address them. He asked them to again pledge themselves to the two Majesties, which they obediently did. Pardo did not tarry long at Juada, and soon he was on his way in search of his sergeant and the road to New Spain. He and his men took the direction of north northwest and probably followed the Indian path that crossed the high mountains over present-day Hog Pen Gap in the northwest Georgia mountains. From the summit of this high mountain ridge, he continued northwest a short distance before arriving at present-day Blairsville, Georgia and continued due west. At the end of four days after leaving Juada, Pardo reached the Indian town of Tocax located on the Toccoa River in the vicinity of Blue Ridge Lake, Georgia. After leaving present-day Georgia into Tennessee, the Toccoa River becomes the Ocoee. Pardo describes Tocax as a very nice town with houses of lumber and having a sizeable population. Vandera tells us that there were grapes, chestnuts, walnuts and other fruit which were better than those of the Sierra Morena of Spain.

On leaving the Toccoa River country, Pardo traveled westerly. After two days, he arrived at another Indian village called Cauchi in the vicinity of Chatsworth, Georgia at the foot of present-day Fort Mountain State Park. Vandera calls it very principal land and that from Cauchi on forward, the land is very rich much like that of Andalusia. Again here, as in all the other Indian towns, the customary speech was made, and the Indians in return swore allegiance to the King and to the Pope. Cauchi was on a principal river which is probably present-day Holly Creek in the vicinity of the junction of Holly Creek and the Conasauga River in Goergia as it begins its swing south along the eastern base of the Appalachian Mountains after a brief run through the southern part of Polk County, Tennessee.

Three days' march down the Conasauga River brought Pardo and his men to an Indian town called Tanasqui, which was probably on the Oostanaula River, a short distance from the junction of Conasauga and Coosawatte Rivers where they come together to form the Oostanaula River and in close proximity to New Ecota, a later day Cherokee Indian capital. Pardo describes Tanasqui as being on a copious river, and the town itself was stockaded and towers built of lumber. Of special interest at this point is to note that Pardo mentions the possibility of the existence of gold and silver at this particular place. As indicated previously, during the Tristan de Luna expedition to that part of Georgia mention was also made of the possibility of gold and silver at or near that very place. Old diggings of mining activities of unknown origin have often been attributed to Spanish presence in that part of Georgia during the sixteenth century. A gold rush occurred a mere fifty miles more or less to the east of Dahlonega, Georgia in the late 1820's and prompted the State of Georgia to appropriate the surrounding lands from the Cherokees. A federal mint operated at Dahlonega from 1838 to 1861.

One more day of travel along the winding Oostanaula River brought the Spaniards to the junction of the Oostanaula and Etowah Rivers to the Indian town of Chiaha located between the two rivers. Vandera gives us a very vivid picture of how the town and its environs appeared during the Fall of 1567. Vandera notes as follows: "It is very rich land, and spacious, it is a large place surrounded by very beautiful rivers; there is in the vicinity of this place, a league or two leagues or three leagues or less or more, many small places (hamlets), all surrounded by rivers; there are some meadows that are heavenly, much grape and very good dedlar trees, in fact, it is a land of Angels."

And it truly must have been. As mentioned previously, it was to this place that Tristan de Luna y Arellano's soldiers had ventured and lived for a brief time, and when they were finally ordered back to Pensacola, they reluctantly obeyed orders. They had found the land and its inhabitants very agreeable. As noted by one of the religious in the advance party, the Indians themselves regretted seeing Arellano's soldiers depart, since not only had the Spaniards treated the Indians well, but they also had provided the Indians with military protection from the more warlike Chiscas of the north. Consequently this kind of comradery between the Spaniards and Chiaha against the Chiscas explains the Chiscas display of enmity toward Bayano and his men less than a decade later following the presence of Arellano's Spaniards in that part of the country. We shall see later in this narrative the same enmity displayed toward Pardo and his party.

Captain Pardo, in his RELACION (official report) to the King pertaining to his activities while in the interior, gives the following account of his arrival at Chiaha and subsequent events until he returned to Santa Elena; "I arrived at Chiaha, which is known by another name, Lameco, where I found Sergeant Bayano and the soldiers at which time they related to me how the Indians had had them divided; and, as such, I had all the Indians and caciques brought together, and I made them the appropriate speech like all the rest.

Figure 13. OVERLOOKING CHIAHA—Chiaha or San Pedro as the Spanish under Juan Pardo called the large Creek town sat where present-day Rome, Georgia is situated. Tristan de Luna y Arellano's men in 1559-60 penetrated this far north during their surveying expedition from Santa Maria de Ichuse, present-day Pensacola, Florida. The purpose of the road-survey was to establish an overland route from the Gulf coast to the Atlantic Seaboard. Arellano was the self-same Capitan Arellano of the Juan Vasques expedition into New Mexico during the early 1540's. Stone ruins of the Spanish fort are visible atop Mt. Alto. The Spanish soldier/settlers depicted in the drawing are looking down on Chiaha from Mt. Alto.

Here I remained eighteen days so that the people would get to know me. It was at this time that I learned through the amicable Indians of how in my line-of-march there were six or seven thousand warriors laying in wait for me which were Carrusa, Chisca, Costehey and Coosa, and in spite of this I decided to continue my travel anyway. I departed in the direction of Zacateccas (New Spain) and the mines of San Martin. I traveled three days from this town (Chiaha) where at the end of three days, I arrived at a town whose name I do not recall, and I gathered the caciques and Indians, and I made the usual speech to them."[13] Vandera remembered the name of the town and states that it took them three days to reach the town, Chalaume, which lay beyond uninhabited country and where they found mountains more rugged than the mountains that were recalled previously. Undoubtedly, Vandera is referring to the country west of present-day Rome, Georgia. They marched past the main ridge of the Appalachian Mountains as the Coosa River, which comes into being at the junction of the Etowah and Oostanaula Rivers, flows from present-day Georgia into Alabama. Chalaume was located somewhere in the vicinity of Fort Payne, Alabama on the west side of Lookout Mountain. Vandera notes that while descending from one of those mountains, they saw smoke from metal, and that Pardo asked his alchemists about it, and they replied with confidence that it was silver.

Pardo's RELACION follows the course of events while in Alabama; "Next day I departed from Chalaume and arrived at Satapo (west of present-day Gadsden) where I found a large congregation of Indians, and there I was not as well-received as I usually was. The cacique hid himself and would not approach me; I, therefore, called his people together so as to tell them that which I would ask of them on behalf of God and of His Majesty. A few gathered on seeing how many we were, however, they did not respond to my harangue even though there were some who understood. And as such that night my interpreters came to me and informed me that they would not go forward with me because it was known that there was a large number of Indians laying in wait for us to cut my throat and those who were with me. And in this manner, an Indian who properly knew what he was talking about approached me. He told me to give him an axe, and then he would reveal to me a thing of great importance. And as such, I gave it to him, and he told me how the Indians of Chisca, Carrass, Coste and Coosa were laying in wait one journey from here (Satapo), and that there were one hundred caciques. On hearing this, I assembled my officers, and we entered into council and agreed that we were no match for so many Indians since they could probably crush us. As such, we decided to give praise to God, and we made the turn to which we returned in four days to Lameco, which was another name of Chiaha. And all this land, as I have said, is very good where Chiaha is, and I made a fort so that Your Majesty could be served. (Pardo named it Fort San Pedro) And as such, there remained there at Chiaha a clergy and thirty soldiers with provisions and firearms."

In addition to leaving tools, Pardo delivered to Marcos Jimenez, fort commander, sixty pounds of powder, eighty-five pounds of lead balls, and fifty pounds of match cord. Pardo also issued shoes and sandals, not only to forty-eight of his own men, but to the leading Indians at Chiaha. The list of men being issued shoes and sandals on October 8, 1567, at Chiaha discloses that those men left behind to man the forts bore either Spanish or Portuguese surnames, i.e. Valdez, Gonzales, Enriques, Romero, Martin, Gallego, Gomes, Morales, Grenon, Canizares, etc.[14] At Chiaha, as he had done in every Indian town along the way, Pardo presented the caciques who came to greet him with gifts. The gifts consisted usually of axes, wedges, chisels, buttons and taffeta. In return, the caciques agreed to build and stock corn cribs for the exclusive use of the Spaniards. At the end of his fifteen day stay at Chiaha, Pardo departed and retraced his journey back to Cauchi.

The men who remained behind were requested to swear before God that under no circumstances would they depart from the fort without orders from high authority. This same procedure was followed at all of the other forts. History has revealed that the Spanish and Portuguese soldier/settlers were true to their oath. All along the way caciques came to ask Pardo that he leave pious ones so that their people could be taught the Faith. At Cauchi there remained twelve soldiers and one catechist in a fort that was built for their protection. The fort was named San Pablo and was adequately supplied by Pardo with both munitions, powder and provisions. Included in the supplies were: thirty-six pounds of lead balls, twenty-two pounds of powder, twenty-four pounds of match cord, two dozen chisels and knives, and a Biscayan axe. Pedro Flores was left in command.[15]

Although the Indians showed signs of being friendly toward the Spaniards and Portuguese, newcomer Pardo felt it wise to fortify and provision other newcomers so that they might be safe from the warlike natives after his own departure. Juan de La Vandera, soldier/notary, while visiting Cauchi in the Fall of 1567 was asked to take note and record the following incident at Cauchi. "After what has been noted previously, on October 3, 1567, the captain (Pardo), being in the town of Cauchi, saw a male Indian mingling among the Indian women with an apron on and doing the chores as the women did. The captain, having observed this, summoned Guillermo Rufin, interpreter, and the other interpreter, and when they were thus summoned, the captain, in front of many soldiers of his company, told the interpreters to ask why that particular Indian went among the Indian women wearing an apron. The interpreters asked the above mentioned cacique of that town, and the cacique replied through the interpreters that the Indian was his brother and that because he was not a man for war nor performing the duties of a man, he went about in that manner like a woman, and he did all that is given to women to do. The captain, having learned the

List of Individuals Who Were Issued Shoes And Sandals At Chiaha by Pardo 1567

Hernando Boyano
Lucas de Canizares
Baltasar
Lope Goncales
Pedro de Bentura
Juan de Castaneda
Francisco Enriques
Lucas Hernandes
Miguel Romano
Juan Carrasco
Matheo Sanches
Juan Lopez
Albaro
Pedro Alonso
Luys de Aguilar
Albaro de Mendana
Juan Martin
Pascuale Lopes
Miguel Sanchez Calero
Juan Perez Domingo Martin
Gabriel de Paniagua
Juan Gallego
Francisco Perez
Pedro Martin de La Carca
Thome Albarez
Alonso Bela
Antonio de Carrion
Alonso Martin
Miguel Goncalez
Domingo Miguelez
Sebastian Comes
Alonso de Aguila
Juan Martin de Olibares
Antonio de Vrito
Pedro Peralta
Diego de Morales
Andres Martin
Anton Munoz
Juan Grenon
Barahona
Pedro Hernan de Rodrigo
Pedro de Sierra
Pedro de Barcena
Xptobal de Villalobos
Alonso de Rojas
Francisco Maldonado
Melchior Melendez
Andres Valdes

Source: AGI, Contratacion 2929 No. 2, R.7

above, commanded me, Juan de La Vandera, notary, to write it in the above form in order that it may be known and understood how war-like the Indians of their provinces of Florida are."[16]

Although Pardo was anxious to continue his journey back to Santa Elena, he remained in Cauchi longer than he had anticipated since many caciques from the surrounding country insisted on visiting with him and receiving the gifts. One such cacique (a female) from the north of Cauchi from the Indian town of Conosaqui (Conasauga) came to pledge her loyalty and accept her gifts of chisels, wedges, necklaces, and taffeta. It was not until November 1, 1567, that Pardo was able to take his leave of Cauchi having satisfied all the visiting Indian leaders and having accepted their usual "Yaa," meaning that they were ready to do His Majesty's bidding.

After Pardo departed from Cauchi, he traveled through mountainous country. After two days, he arrived at Tocax where he was again greeted by friendly caciques and other Indians who in turn gave Pardo the usual "Yaa." After a two day stay at Tocax, Pardo and his dwindling force set out for Juada which they reached in four days. Again, as at the other Cherokee towns along the way, large numbers of Indians and their caciques greeted the Spaniards on their arrival at Juada or Cuenca, the Spanish name given to the new settlement. Pardo spoke to them the customary speech, and they agreed to allegiance to His Majesty. He left Alferez Alberto Escudero de Villamar with thirty soldiers at Fort San Juan so that he could have contact with the other forts which were built in the neighboring towns so that from there he could give support to the soldiers remaining in the part of the mountains, Cauchi and Chiaha.[17]

For defensive purposes, Pardo delivered to Villamar sixty-eight pounds of matchcord, one hundred pounds of lead balls, and eighty-five pounds of powder. In addition to the implements of war, Captain Pardo also supplied the Cuenca settlement with thirty-four pounds of nails, forty-two large chisels for hewing logs, three iron shovels, two socketed axes, four iron wedges, two hoes and two pickaxes. Villamar was asked to swear before God that he would remain at Cuenca and hold the land unless ordered to leave by the King or other high authority.

Pardo remained ten days in Juada, as he had another place to visit. He departed in the direction of Guatari, or Salamanca, its Spanish name, and he remained there four days. On arriving, Pardo found the Indians and caciques together, and he made the customary speech to them, and they responded that they were ready to do that which His Holiness and His Majesty ordered. They asked Pardo to leave religious ones and as such, the Spaniards built a fort where he left sixteen soldiers and a clergyman, Father Sebastian Montero, with them.[18]

The fort was of raised earth and wood. At each corner stood tall cavaliers constructed with thick wood. Between the cavaliers ran a high wall of poles and dirt. Lucas de Canizares was left in command of Fort Santiago. He was asked to swear that he would not leave Salamanca until his Grace, or someone in His Majesty's name, should command it. Pardo further ordered Canizares that no one should dare to bring any women into the fort at night and that he should not depart from the command under pain of being severely punished. Pardo gave and delivered to Lucas de Canizares: fifty-one pounds of lead, thirty-four pounds of match cord, thirty-four pounds of powder, and miscellaneous tools for working logs.

After a sixteen day stay at Guatari, Pardo departed for Santa Elena which he reached on March 2, 1568, having been on the road for more than six months. Thus, Captain Pardo departed from the interior lands of South Carolina, Georgia, Tennessee and Alabama never to return as he and the Adelantado, Pedro Menendez, became involved in many other pursuits in the service of the King. But what of the more than ninety Spaniards and Portuguese who were left behind in the remote Appalachian Mountains among the Cherokee,

Figure 14. DEEP IN THE WILDERNESS ALONG THE CHATTAHOOCHEE—The Spanish soldier/settlers are enjoying a cool refreshing drink fom the mountain waters of the Chattahoochee River in the northern mountains of present-day Georgia. Juan Pardo established his settlement of Cuenca not far from this spot.

Creek and Catawba Indians? As many as seventeen and thirty-six years later there was still a Spanish record of their presence in the isolated settlements of the interior. In one such settlement there was an account written about the fate which befell one such group of Spaniards. The account or *Relacion* dated in 1584 tells of an Indian attack on one of the settlements. It relates that a male Spaniard (a fifer), his wife and his daughter survived the attack and were still in the interior. In 1598, a Spanish expedition reached the vicinity of Stone Mountain, Georgia. They were informed by an Indian cacique that four days' travel toward the north lived men such as they who wore their hair short, used axes to fell down trees, and lived in houses. Undoubtedly many of the original Spanish soldier/settlers of the second Pardo expedition were single men, and it was not an uncommon event for a Spanish soldier, while stationed in a remote area to take an Indian wife.

A race of Indian and European mixture thus emerged in the Southeastern United States. A race which essentially still exists to this day. Although the trace of American Indian blood after almost fifteen generations has dimmed in the genetic chain according to a 1969 gene frequency analysis of almost 200 Melungeons. The new race of Cherokee and Spanish, Catawba and Spanish, Creek and Spanish developed a subculture. As each successive generation passed, they married only within the subculture, and began to progressively function outside of the pure Indian world. Later when the Irish and English arrived on the scene in the mountains of Georgia, South Carolina, Tennessee, North Carolina and Virginia this melange would also function outside of the English and later the American world as well. More than ninety Spaniards and Portuguese remained in the mountains of northern Georgia and northeastern South Carolina a few miles from Tennessee and North Carolina. These ninety men would have been sufficient to begin a new race of people. Thus the Melungeons.

When the first English men first came over the mountains from North Carolina and Virginia, they took note of a certain peoples who occupied land in the mountains of eastern Tennessee and southwestern Virginia. John Sevier, one of the earliest pioneers to enter eastern Tennessee and its mountains in the early 1770's, noted that the high ridges and valleys of what is today Hancock and Rhea Counties, Tennessee were occupied by a distinctive people who were neither Indian nor Negro. Sevier noted that they had fine European features although they had dark skins of reddish-brown complexion. These people claimed, at that time, to be of Iberian origin. Sevier does not go on to state the nature of their origins other than to state that these dark complexioned people claimed to be Portuguese or as they themselves stated "Porterghee." It should be noted that John Sevier, himself, was of Spanish origins. The Seviers or Javiers were native to Navarre, Spain and came to New Market, Virginia by way of France and England. Juan Javier's (John Sevier) father was Valentino Javier or Xavier as it is oftentimes written.[19] The coat-of-arms depicts a Moorish youth in the upper right quadrant. Juan Javier of the 1770's had more in common with the reddish-brown Melungeons than he realized. One wonders if John Sevier would have been elected Governor of Tennessee had he gone by his Spanish name. Javier was not the first to observe these people. One such group, a party of men sent out in the early 1700's by the governor of Virginia to explore the "uncharted wilderness" of the far distant mountains toward the west, came across a family of non-Indians living in a very comfortable house and farming the land in the vicinity of present-day Pound, Virginia a few miles west of Norton and Wise, Virginia. The party noted that it appeared that those people had been living there for quite sometime.

Over a period of time the name by which these people became known as a distinct group was Melungeon. The most probable source of the term Melungeon is from the French word melange, meaning a mixture or medley. The word Melungeon is obviously an adaptation of the French word Melangeon. The French first arrived in Tennessee in western Tennessee in the vicinity of Memphis during the late 1600's during La Salle's first descent of the Mississippi when he established Fort Prudonne on the Wolf River. Later, French trappers made their way into the Nashville Basin in search of furs and to trade with the native Americans. As early as 1714 there was a French trading post on the site of present-day Nashville or Nashboro as it was previously called. These Frenchmen plied their trade between French Fort and eastern Tennessee and came in contact with the dark-skinned reddish-brown complexioned people who were neither Indian nor Negro, but had fine European features, i.e. the term melange or more specifically melanger meaning "mixed breed." Melungeons have historically denied having Negroid blood, preferring to think of themselves as Indian mixed with European and by their own claims "Porterghee." A more recent explanation of the term Melungeon is that it comes from Melungo, an Afro-Portuguese word meaning "white person." The term "white person" was probably used by the Moors to distinguish between themselves and the Spanish/ Portuguese occupants of the Iberian Peninsula. The Moors were comprised of people of Berber and Arab origins who occupied most of Spain and Portugal from the eighth century until the fifteenth century. The Berbers, it should be noted, were of a reddish complexion. They occupied those lands along the southern shores of the Mediterranean in northwest Africa. Their dark skins, however, have been the cause of racial discrimination for generations of Melungeons. The State of Tennessee in 1796 in its constitution granted every freeman, regardless of color, full citizenship rights. Then in 1834 , the State of Tennessee limited those rights, using the "color barrier" as a de facto way of taking away the vote and other rights of the Melungeons. It was years before their full rights would be restored. However, even though their constitutional rights were in time restored, these particular peoples continued to be subjected to indignities inherent to racial discrimination at its worst.

In his book, *Almost White*, Brewton Berry includes a direct quote from a Melungeon woman who depicts the situation with which the Melungeons were subjected: "Early in the last century (1800) when the white folks first came here, the Melungeons was already here, a 'hold' all the good land, but didn't want to just take from the Melungeons brutal-like. Well, it wouldn't a been no trouble if the Melungeons was ordinary heathen Indians. They woulda 'just kicked' em out. But there they was sorta 'livin' liked civilized folks and they was 'speakin' English, an 'on top o' all that they was believin Christians. But their skins was brown on account 'o' their Injun blood in 'em' too. Then they passed a law saying 'nobody with nigger blood could vote, or hold office, or testify in court.' Then they went to court and before long they got hold 'o' that good bottom land. So there wasn't nothin left for the Melungeons to do but move up on the ridges."

One such ridge, Newman Ridge, lies to the west of present-day Sneedville, Tennessee and over the years has had the highest concentration of Melungeons. Another high concentration of Melungeons can be found further north along the northern extension of Newman Ridge high in the Cumberland Plateau in the Norton and Wise, Virginia vicinity. Today many descendants of the Melungeons continue to reside in and around Sneedville, Tennessee and Wise, Virginia, but the question of their origins has not been satisfactorily answered. During the past two centuries numerous theories have surfaced, however, they remain simply that, theories. The crux of the matter is that no historian or researcher has been able to provide verifiable historical data which places significant numbers of Europeans in the general vicinity of the Melungeon communities prior to the coming of the French, Scot-Irish and English into the mountains of northwestern South Carolina, western

North Carolina, northeastern Georgia and eastern Tennessee. Spaniards were in that part of the southeastern United States as early as 1540 when De Soto made his pass through the above mentioned areas. However, it is not likely that the Melungeons are descendant from De Soto's Spaniards since the number of deserters from Soto's ranks were few. There was, however, another group of intrepid Spaniards who came to those mountains of Georgia near Helen, Rome and Chatsworth, Georgia and in the rolling, green hills of South Carolina along the Wateree River south of Rock Hill, South Carolina.

Initially the Spaniards lived in close proximity to the forts and settlement towns that Pardo ordered built so as to hold the land for King Felipe II who had hopes of building an overland route from Santa Maria de Ichuse (present-day Pensacola, Florida) to Santa Elena (present-day Beaufort, South Carolina). The men in these settlements were ordered to remain in the forts and towns and to protect the Indians who embraced the Holy Roman Faith. Those men remained at their isolated mountain outposts and were not recalled back to Santa Elena. In addition to those Spaniards of Pardo's expedition who stayed in the interior and raised families in the frontier wilderness, other Spaniards and their families had already lived in Virginia in the interior for two generations. As previously noted in an earlier chapter, some of Lucas Vasquez de Ayllon's colonists left the 1526 colony of San Miguel de Guandape taking their families with them into the interior. Both Raleigh's and John Smith's people mentioned non-Indian people living in the interior of Virginia south of Jamestown and west of Roanoke.

There is evidence, as noted previously, that some if not most of Pardo's men married Indian women of the Cherokee, Creek, and Catawba tribes. It is not unlikely then that once the children of these Spaniards and Portuguese began to multiply in numbers, a separate culture, a more European than Indian culture emerged. Consequently, these "mixed breeds" were forced to function outside of the Indian culture and relocated to territories outside of the local Indian tribes. Thus the migration to the isolated valleys of northern North Carolina, Tennessee, southwestern Virginia and eastern Kentucky occurred. The lands into which most members of this new race/culture migrated was along the northern and eastern boundary of the Yuchi Indians (Chiscas as the Spaniards called them) who had previously occupied the Tennessee Valley and its tributaries north of Chattanooga, Tennessee. The Yuchis were of the Siouan linguistic stock while the Cherokee were of the southern Iroquoian linguistic stock. Another very prominent tribe in that part of the southeastern United States, the Creeks, were of the Muskhogean stock. The Spaniards dealt on amicable terms primarily with the Cherokees, Creeks and Catawbas in the mountains of the Carolinas, Georgia, and Tennessee. The Yuchis for one reason or another as previously noted declared themselves enemies of the Spaniards. The reason for the Yuchis' departure from the Tennessee Valley is not known. Within a few years after the arrival of Europeans, they were no longer to be found in the Tennessee River Valley nor in the mountains of eastern Tennessee. After leaving eastern Tennessee, the Yuchis moved eastward into South Carolina and Georgia, and at a later date they allied themselves with the Yamasses and English to make war on the Spaniards. The lands which they had formerly occupied in Tennessee were left vacant. It was during this time, then, that the Melungeons found it opportune to move into eastern Tennessee. It was in those mountains that the French during the early 1700's and later during the late 1700's that people from the United States, John Sevier (Juan Javier) being one of them found them not up on the high ridges, but in the lowlands along the rivers. It was later, as more and more Scot-Irish settlers moved into these regions in large enough numbers and coveted the bottom lands, that the Melungeons sought refuge in the high ridges on land that nobody wanted.

Although many of these people have married non-Melungeons and have moved out of the isolated mountain ridges, and others have left home for jobs in the industrialized cities of the Midwest, a walk along the streets of Sneedville, Tennessee or a visit to the public library in Wise, Virginia, or most towns and villages in eastern Kentucky reveals that the Melungeon strain is still very much in evidence. In July of 1984, I visited Sneedville and Newman Ridge for the first time. I am from the southwestern United States where Spaniards under Juan de Onate came to settle the Kingdom of New Mexico in 1598. Although during the succeeding four centuries descendants of those Spaniards brought their families with them, many others took Indian wives and their offspring acquired the characteristics of both cultures, Indian and European. During my visit to Hancock County, I was struck by the sameness of appearance and characteristics of residents of Espanola or Las Vegas, New Mexico or for that matter almost any town located north of Albuquerque, New Mexico with those people of Sneedville. I was not the only individual in the party struck by the similarities. My twelve year old daughter, Alicia, accompanied me on that trip to Sneedville, as well as did my father and mother who were on a short vacation from New Mexico. Somewhere along the way from Knoxville, Tennessee heading for Sneedville as we wound our way over mountain ridges and along the narrow valleys, or hallows as they are more commonly called in Tennessee, Alicia fell asleep. As I was maneuvering my automobile into a parking space in front of the Hancock County Courthouse, Alicia awakened, and her first words, as she peered half-asleep out of the car window at the people milling about the courthouse or strolling along the sidewalks were: "What are we doing in Las Vegas?" Meaning Las Vegas, New Mexico where we had lived during the later part of the 1970's. My father and mother were also struck by the "likeness" of faces similar to those of northern New Mexico. My father, "A Man of Letters," passed away in 1996. My mother presently close to ninety years of age still holds a fascination for those people in Tennessee who resembled those of her native New Mexico.

As I walked into the courthouse, the first person that I encountered was the county clerk, one Scott Collins. One look at Scott Collins satisfied forever my feeling that the Melungeons were of Spanish origins. He was a "dead-ringer" for any Spanish office holder in any courthouse in northern New Mexico. I did not ask Scott if he was a Melungeon nor did he tell me, but I knew at that moment that he was indeed a person of my own Spanish heritage. Scott Collins today is a credit to that heritage and a good friend and associate in the search for Melungeon origins. Without realizing the significance of her words, Alicia had made the connection between the Spaniards of Pardo's time and the Melungeons of eastern Tennessee. She was gazing with half-closed eyes at the descendants of those hardy men of Spain who were left behind to hold the land for their King. Alicia's own descendants would themselves in a mere three decades in 1598 journey north with Don Juan de Onate to the Kingdom of New Mexico to establish a settlement of Spaniards in those faraway lands. They, too, came to hold the land for their King, and they did indeed hold the land for their King for more than two-and-one-quarter centuries in Santa Fe, New Mexico.

Recently I came across a study on the blood types of almost two hundred Melungeons in east Tennessee and southwestern Virginia. The findings of that study show, using advanced technological procedures, that those people are of Western Mediterranean origins and most probably from the Iberian Peninsula. More on that later. A separate chapter will be devoted to the descendants of Pardo's and Ayllon's men and their struggle to survive in that lonely place between the light and the dark races.

Part III
THE HERITAGE—ORIGINS OF THE IBERIANS

i

The origins of the peoples of the Iberian Peninsula (Spanish/Portuguese) are many and varied. For this reason when one is asked what does a Melungeon look like, the answer can be as varied as the origins of the Iberians themselves. A family of Melungeons for example can have members vary, one member can be small, wiry, dark-complexioned; another light colored eyes (blue or hazel), fair skin and hair; another blue eyes and very blond hair; another relatively light complexioned, heavy (burly), chestnut hair sometimes curly. I have visited families in the Louisiana Redbone and Virginia Melungeons communities and have observed these family characteristics where the offspring have the same facial features except for their coloring and hair texture. Sadly, it has been my observation that when the offspring differ in coloring, they also differ in self-confidence and social forwardness. The darker complexioned offspring are more hesitant to come forward socially as though fearful that they are less socially acceptable than their light-colored siblings. In many of the Melungeon, Redbone, Lumbee etc. communities, when asked to explain their non-Anglo appearance, they call themselves, Black Dutch, Black Irish, Portuguese, and in more recent years Cherokee, not Indian but Cherokee. Only recently I visited with a long-time associate who at one time called himself Black Dutch. Since discovering that the Melungeons came from a very honorable and heroic past, he as many others of Melungeon heritage no longer hide behind the Black Dutch, Black Irish shield. Recently he acknowledged to me that "its not so bad being Spanish."

What then does it mean to be Spanish/Portuguese (Iberian)? To attempt to distinguish between Portuguese and Spanish, except for dialect, is like attempting to distinguish between a Tennessean and a Virginian. The division is a political subdivision, not a genetic subdivision. Portugal or Portus Cale as the Romans called the Atlantic side of the Iberian Peninsula was up until 1143 A.D. part of the western-counties of the Kingdom of Leon in Galicia in northwestern Spain. It was only after Henry of Burgundy with the permission of the Spanish King and promise that he could rule over all those western lands along the Atlantic seaboard which he could reclaim from the Moors that Portus Cale became the Country of Portugal. Henry of Burgundy whose mother was the Spanish King's daughter achieved success beyond his wildest expectations in driving out the Moors. Indeed, Henry of Burgundy was so successful that he proclaimed himself "King" and petitioned the then Roman Catholic Pope to recognize his reconquered lands, i.e. Portus Cale, as a sovereign nation, ergo the Country of Portugal.[1] Even today the ties between Galicians and Portuguese are very close. The language called Portuguese comes primarily from Galiciano Spanish. The present-day Portuguese term for Galicia is Gallego. I am a Gallego as were many of Pardo's men. The earliest description of my ancestor, Antonio Gallegos, who came from Galicia to help settle the New Mexico colony in the early 1600's and late 1500's was "tall, angular nose, blond hair and wore a reddish beard." On the other hand on my mothers side, one Bernardo Gonzales was born in Lisboa, Portugal, came to New Mexico in the late 1500's and early 1600's. He was described as "short, ruddy and wore a chestnut colored beard." Both came from the same general area of the Iberian Peninsula, yet both were very different in their physical appearance and complexion.

Just as the United States is often times referred to as the "melting pot" of North America, so was the Iberian Peninsula the "melting pot" of Europe which is what gives the Spanish and Portuguese peoples their Indo-European or Aryan origins. However, the Iberian Peninsula belongs neither to Europe nor to Africa, but to both. In referring to Africa, it is meant not the lower part of the Continent peopled by black men, but the northern lands of the Dark Continent north of the Atlas Mountains and south of the shores of the Mediterranean in the old territories of the Mauritanian Empire. The term Moor comes from Mauri which was what the Spanish called the peoples of the ancient Berber Empire. It was from North Africa that the first historically identifiable peoples came to the Iberian Peninsula. The ancient Iberians possibly as early as 3000 B.C. crossed the Straits of Gibraltar to people present-day Spain/ Portugal. The towering Pyrenees along the present-day Spanish Franco frontier restricted these ancient peoples' movements farther north into the rest of Europe. The Iberians were a small, wiry, dark-complexioned race, great riders of horses and very tribalistic and clannish. Early in the twelfth century, the Phoenicians, a Semitic race of the Canaanite branch came to trade and many stayed. The cities of Cadiz and Malaga were founded by these traders from the eastern Mediterranean as early as 1100 B.C. The Celts, a Nordic race from the north of Europe came in two great waves, the first in 900 B.C. and the second in 600 B.C. The Celts occupied the northern portion of the peninsula above the Ebro River, although many drifted farther south to mix with people already occupying those southern climes. They too came and stayed thus another ingredient was added to the Iberian/ Phoenician/Celtic mixture. The Celts left a distinct physical imprint on the peoples of northern Spain and Portugal. In these areas of Spain there is still today a high percentage of light-colored eyes and very fair skin and hair. Galicia and Asturias on the Bay of Biscay are noted for their blonde types. In Aragon almost 35 percent of the population falls into the fair-skinned, very light-eyed group. As one continues farther south both the shading of the skin and coloration of the eyes darken.

The Greek were the next to arrive in Spain. They came around 600 B.C. and although most of them settled along the Mediterranean coast, some of them also traded along the Bay of Biscay in northern Spain. They like the others before them brought their own unique contributions and characteristics. Like the others before them, they also stayed, thus the Melange (mixture) grows, i.e. Iberian/Phoenician/Celtic/Greco. Next to arrive and stay were the Carthaginians from the shores of North Africa around Tunisia and Algeria. Probably the most noted Spanish/Carthaginian was Hannibal who wreaked havoc in Roman Italy. Very close on the Carthaginians' heels were the Romans in 209 B.C. when the Roman legion under Publius Comelius Scipio (Africanus) captured the Carthaginian base at Cartagena in 209 B.C. It was not until 19 B.C., however, before Roman rule was established throughout the entire peninsula. As the others before them, they too stayed, thus the Melange grew, i.e. Iberian/Phoenician/Celtic/Greco/Carthaginian /Italian. During Roman times in Spain and Portugal, Jews began to enter Spain in large numbers. Starting in the reign of Hadrian (117 A.D.-138 A.D.) and increasing among the Antonines. According to Jewish legend the ancient Hebrews had established colonies there many hundreds of years before the time of Christ in Nebuchadnezzar's time.

As the Roman Empire began to fall, Germanic tribes began to enter the Iberian Peninsula. In 409 A.D. the Vandals were the first to pour into the peninsula. The Suevi and Alani also invaded Spain, however, they came in smaller numbers. The Vandals being more numerous overran the entire peninsula but settled mostly in southern Spain thus the name Andalusia (Vandalusia or Land of the

Vandal) given to the land by the invading Arabs three centuries later in 711 A.D. The Vandals ravaged the country and were excessively brutal, thus the term "vandalism." The Vandals had hardly established themselves when a fourth Germanic tribe, the semi-civilized Visigoths overran Spain putting the Vandals and the other Germanic tribes to "heels." The Visigoths having had some contact with the Romans in Germany became partially Romanized and largely Christian and by around 600 A.D. established a dynasty in Spain which lasted until the final wave of invaders, the Arabs, defeated the Visigoths in 711 A.D., thus the final input to the Melange was in place, i.e. Iberian/Phoenician/Celtic/Greco/Carthaginian/Italian/Jewish/Vandal/Visigoth/Moorish. The term Moor came from the Latin Mauri of the Mauritanian Empire. Those peoples included in the generic Moor were Arabs, Berbers and Turks.

When the Spanish/Portuguese soldiers and colonists came to settle in the New World, they came with the Melange already a part of them. There were no Turkish Turks, no Jews, no Arabs or Berbers coming from Spain to settle the King's New World colonies. Those allowed to come were Spanish and Portuguese Catholics, be they born Catholic or converted Catholics (conversos or Moriscos). All the elements needed to complete the Melange except American Indian had come together to form a new culture outside of the Anglo world. The Isolates, the mysterious peoples of the Southeastern United States divided as follows from their Iberian base:

BASE

SPANISH/PORTUGUESE

MELUNGEONS	**RED BONES**	**TURKS**	**BRASS ANKLES**	**LUMBEES**
Tennessee	S. Car.	S. Car.	S. Car.	N. Car.
Virginia	Louisiana		N. Car.	
Alabama				
Kentucky				
Georgia				

Of the above, the Melungeons are the most numerous and most widespread. In addition they are also the most studied and debated. Over a period of more than 300 years other people coming into the interior of the Southeastern United States have speculated and theorized concerning the mysterious peoples' origins, however, it has only been during the past one hundred-plus years that writers, researchers, and anthropologists have done serious work on the subject. Burnett (1889) theorized that the Melungeons were a tri-racial hybrid of poor white-trash, runaway black slaves and renegade Indians. Small wonder that the Melungeons went underground rather than live that inglorious heritage. Next to write about the Melungeons was Dromgoole (1891) who claimed to recognize Cherokee, African, English and Portuguese/Spanish surnames in the group. However, Melungeons are reported to disclaim any Black heritage considering themselves to be mainly of Portuguese descent. Droomgoole traced a branch of a Melungeon family to a man named Denhan, reputedly a Portuguese, said to have come from one of the Spanish settlements farther south, who settled on Mulberry Creek where he married a sister of the first

Solomon Collins. Dromgoole also mentions a blacksmith on Blackwater Creek north of Sneedville, Tennessee whom he visited while in the Sneedville/Newman Ridge vicinity. According to Dromgoole this blacksmith was "dark as a genuine African," yet there was a peculiar tinge to his complexion that was totally foreign to the Black Race. The Blacksmith had a white wife, a Mullins woman, a descendant of English and Indian. The man, himself, was a Denhan, a grandson of the old Portuguese emigrant and a Collins woman. In the Hawkins County tax list of 1810 there was listed a John Denhan, noted as "white."[2]

Henriette Mertz (1976) presented the case for Portuguese immigration to Florida in 734 A.D. to escape the Moors. Rollin Gillespie (1986) postulated that the Melungeons are descended from Milesians, the founders of Milan, who fled their Anatolian homeland at the time of its invasion by Persians in 492 B.C. Gillespie suggests that most of the Milesians went to Ireland by way of their trading colony at Cadiz, Spain, but that one contingent went to the island of Melun in the Seine. He relates Caesar's difficulty in driving the "Melungeons" from their island stronghold in 52 B.C. and suggests that some escaped to America. Another pre-Columbian theory suggests that the Melungeons are white Indian descendants from Prince Modoc of Wales. None of the pre-Columbian origins can be substantiated by verifiable historical data.

The first published scientific data relating to the genetic make-up of Melungeons, *Survey of Demography, Anthropology, and Genetics In The Melungeons of Tennessee* by William H. Brown and William S. Pollitzer, anthropologists, appeared in print in 1969. The anthropologists (Pollitzer and Brown) studied measurement of skin, color, hair, form, cephalic index, and gene frequencies in six blood group systems from 177 Melungeons of Hancock County, Tennessee and Lee County, Virginia. Their findings were in line with those expected of a Caucasoid population, with little evidence of Negroid or American Indian influence.[3]

In 1972, Pollitzer followed up with *The Physical Anthropology and Genetics of Marginal People of The Southeastern United States*. In his 1972 paper, Pollitzer suggests a people who are ninety percent white, almost ten percent Indian and relatively little Negro, if any, in their origins according to the gene frequency analysis. These percentages are based, however, on hypothetical hybrids assuming that the Melungeons are basically English. However the actual genetic data gathered does not support the "English" assumption nor does the gene frequency analysis conducted at a later date. Pollitzer and Brown also state that the Melungeons appear to be more Caucasoid and less Negroid than other isolates studied and far less Indian than the admixed Catawbas of South Carolina.[4]

In 1990, James L. Guthrie, using data from the blood samples taken by Pollitzer and Brown in the late 1960's reevaluated the gene frequencies using modern technological advances in genetics and the genetic chain. Instead of six blood groups, Guthrie compared data from five blood groups which included thirty-six world populations. Guthrie, like the others before him, concluded that the Melungeon pattern of the four combinations in the MNSs system (MS, Ms, NS, Ns) indicates a Caucasoid population. The Haptoglobin (Hp)data narrows this somewhat, pointing to a European, and probably to a Southern European or Mediterranean origin. A Black or American Indian influence is counter-indicated. For example the worldwide values of Hp range from 3-95 percent. Europeans average about 40 percent; higher in the north and lower in the south. The Melungeon value is 38.5 percent. The lowest values occur in India and east Asia; the highest in Black Africa, Oceania, and parts of Australia. The range for U.S. whites is 38-40 percent. The range for U.S. Blacks is 53-75. Most American Indians have very high values.[5]

Values of Fy^a in the Duffy system tend to rule out much of an American Indian component. The Melungeon Fy^a value is closest to those of people now living in coastal Europe, north Africa, the Mediterranean islands, the Levant, and to certain populations of Arabia, India, Africa, and eastern Europe. In the Rhesus system, the Melungeon level of the cDe (R^o) haplotype, a marker for Black African ancestry is slightly higher than for most European populations. This should not necessarily be taken for a slight Black American contribution to the Melungeon, since it is typical of many Mediterranean peoples because of long contact with Africa. For example, the Melungeon value for cDe is 9.6 percent, whereas few groups without a known Black component exceed three percent. Range for U.S. Blacks is 24-46 percent. For U.S. Whites the cDe value is 1-6 percent. However, several populations of Italy, Portugal, Spain, and France have values in the range of 9-10 percent.

During the Summer of 1993, Dr. Anthony F. Gallegos, a pioneer in decoding the genetic chain, was privileged to Guthrie's study. His comments are as follows: "The statistical study of phenotypic traits exhibited by the Melungeons clearly corroborates what has been suspected by those who have studied this group (and by the Melungeons themselves) that they originated from a specific Mediterranean group in and around western Spain and Portugal. That the Melungeons also compare well with other groups in the southern Mediterranean region is not surprising since there was a great deal of gene flow in Spain, Portugal, Italy and other proximal locations between Moslems and Jews with the native populations during long periods of time. I had the opportunity of observing the physical appearance (phenotypes) of a small sample of Melungeon people from photographs. In my opinion they have phenotypes that could relate to some groups of Spaniards, Portuguese, Sephardic Jews, and Arabs (Moors). An important factor which seems to have been overlooked in the interpretations is the process of Sewall Wright genetic drift which might have occurred with this group under conditions of a small initial breeding population and geographical and/or social isolation. If this has occurred in the Melungeon group, then it would be expected that certain traits have become established in this population at a higher frequency than that of the parent population (which had already or was in the process of establishing Hardy-Weinberg equilibrium at the time of isolation), and that other traits have either declined or disappeared in the present Melungeon group. This is not an uncommon phenomenon as it has occurred with other population groups in this country and world-wide when such conditions prevent gene flow from the larger parent group.

I asked Dr. A. F. Gallegos to comment on the possibility of refining the results of the gene frequency analysis through DNA testing in conjunction with the Human Genome Project. Dr. Gallegos stated: "You also mentioned that a genotype (DNA) study is being considered for the Melungeons, and asked if I might comment on that. Assuming that over 99 percent of the DNA in all human population groups is identical (much of which is redundant or unused) then such a study would have to concentrate on very small differences. The Human Genome Project supported by U.S. government funding is an indication of the importance of chromosome mapping of human genes for possible use in correcting genetic dysfunctions and addressing the cure of certain diseases. If the study is to address gene frequencies, then it reverts back into the same phenotypic approach, but which might include traits which are not phenotypically observable in the usual sense. Obviously, this all depends on the degree of homozygosity or heterozygosity inherent in the Melungeon group, notwithstanding the genetic drift argument alluded to earlier. If this group contains a significant component of homozygous recessive traits which might be expected to result from an initial small isolated breeding population, then more phenotypic studies might be useful in relating them to suspected parent populations, but I am not sure how DNA studies using both sets of chromosomes will produce any more conclusive information in pinpointing the origins of the Melungeons." Dr. Gallegos' concluding remarks included; "Overall, I believe the gene frequency approach taken to resolve Melungeon origins is the best available given the limited funding and time available for the project, however, it is equally important to support gene frequency studies with historical, cultural, linguistic, and archaeological information which might be obtained from the Melungeon group. Finally, a study of human values traits of this group...etc. world-view, religious aspirations, motivational traits, eccentric and habitual behavior, and idiosyncrasies could be used in support of establishing Melungeon origins when compared to other world population groups."

As stated earlier the gene frequency statistics pertain to a small population (177) in predominantly Melungeon communities. Although the Melungeons are the most publicized of the Southeastern Isolates, the other isolates, i.e. Red Bones, Turks, Brass Ankles and Lumbees have had significant impact on their regional areas.

In their 1969 paper, Pollitzer and Brown suggest that the Melungeons appear to be more Caucasoid and less Negroid than other isolates studied and far less Indian than the admixed Catawbas although to the author's knowledge the same test, i.e. gene frequency comparisons, were made only for the Hancock County, Tennessee and Lee County, Virginia isolates.

Table I which follows is based on information taken from the 1990 James L. Guthrie study.

TABLE I[6]
MEAN MEASURE OF DIVERGENCE (MMD) OF MELUNGEONS FROM OTHER POPULATIONS

POPULATION	MMD
Libya (Tripoli)*	0.017
Cyprus (Troodos-Greek)	0.017
Malta*	0.018
Canary Islands (Spanish)	0.019
Italy (Veneto)	0.022 Close Matches
Portugal	0.024
Italy (Trentino)	0.026
Spain (Galicia)	0.027
U.S. Whites (Minnesota)+	0.028
Ireland#	0.029
Italy	0.030
Sweden	0.030
Libya (minus Fezzan)	0.030
Germany	0.031
Britain	0.031
Greece	0.032
Netherlands	0.032
Wales	0.033
Corsica	0.034
France	0.035
Spain	0.036
U.S. Whites	0.036
England	0.040
Sicily	0.040
Iceland	0.041
Northern Ireland	0.042
Finland	0.046
Sardinia	0.051
Turkey	0.053
Cyprus	0.058
Catawba (mixed)	0.108
U S. Blacks	0.189 Distant Matches
Gullas (Blacks South Carolina)	0.222
Seminole, Oklahoma	0.241
Cherokee	0.256
Seminole, Florida	0.308

Author's Notes for Table I on previous page:

1. A perfect match to Melungeon would be 0.000
2. * The Arab/Berber (Moorish) component of the Spanish/Portuguese of today.
3. + Probably Swedes. Could reflect the Moorish in Swedes.
4. # Married into Melungeon families in S.E. U.S. Does not include Northern Ireland.

The Turks of Sumter County, South Carolina, are not really Turks, at least not in the sense that Turks from Turkey or from any other Arab nation came to settle in the Southeastern United States in a body politic. The Turks of South Carolina in and around Stateburg are called Turks simply because someone observed that they looked Turkish. Actually the term to describe two of the individuals who were the progenitors of the Stateburg isolates was "Caucasians of Arab descent," thus Moors, thus Turks. The account of how these two individuals of Mediterranean appearance, Scott and Benehaly, came to settle in and about Stateburg, South Carolina is well known history, at least to the people of Sumter County. What is virtually unknown is how they and others like them, i.e. Red Bones, Brass Ankles, Lumbees, happened to be that deep in the interior of the Southeastern United States, generations prior to the War of the American Revolution, when Revolutionary War General, Thomas Sumter of South Carolina first came upon Scott and Benenhaly at a country cross-roads. Prior to the War of the American Revolution, General Sumter established himself high up the Santee River on land which he had acquired from the Indians. Shortly after the commencement of hostilities between the colonies and Mother England, General Sumter enlisted many residents of the area as well as friendly Indians in the fight for independence. During one of his recruiting trips north and west of the Santee he came upon a crowd of rough-looking men fighting game chickens at a country crossroads. He harangued them that they might join him in the fight for freedom. Someone in the crowd being impressed by the speech called out, "Boys, that's the blue hen's chicken. He is the gamecock." From that day on, the nickname followed General Sumter wherever he went. One recruit was one Joseph Benenhaley who had the look of an Arab about him. Both he and Scott, the only other recruit mentioned by name, were dark complexioned very unlike the English settlers of that part of South Carolina. General Sumter believed most of the men at the crossroads to be of Arab descent from the coast of North Africa, then part of the Turkish empire, so that they became known as Turks or Moors. Benenhaley became the chief of scouts for General Sumter and Scott the General's bugler. After the War, most of the "Turks" including Scott and Benenhaley, settled around Sumter's plantation. Some of them acquired land and became farmers, however, most of them preferred "life in the wild" and became hunters and trappers.[7]

In 1791, shortly after the ratification of the United States Constitution by South Carolina, these people, calling themselves free citizens of Moorish descent petitioned the South Carolina legislature to be governed by the more generous laws pertaining to white inhabitants and not by the very limited rights provided to slaves and free Negroes. A committee of the legislature sustained their claim to be classified as "white" rather than free person of color (FPC), recommending that they not be subjected to the very stringent prohibitions against Negroes whether free or slaves although this did not keep them free from racial discrimination. The "white" people of the community did not wish to socialize with the Turks nor did they wish for their children to attend school with the darker complexioned children. A federal district judge ordered the Turks into the grade schools in September of 1953. The "white" parents boycotted classes and the judge withdrew the order. The Turks went back to the court, however, it was not until eight years later that they were again admitted to the schools. The basic problem being that even though they had regular Caucasian features, they were perceived by the "white" community as being Negroid.[8] School Board lawyers introduced old census reports to illustrate that some Turks were once listed as "free persons of color." In 1928, a writer for the Columbia Star wrote in defense of these people: "Their skin, though dark, is thin, showing a rosy tint in the cheeks of the young people. Their features are decidedly Caucasian, their ankles and wrists slender, and their insteps arched. No flat feet, flat noses, thick lips, or curly hair are found among them."

The Turks, however, are not the only dark-complexioned isolates which have traditionally resided in that part of South Carolina and eastward into some parts of North Carolina. Not all of the dark-complexioned men which General Sumter recruited settled near the General's plantation, as many of them went back to their own homes after the War of The Revolution. Those who returned to their own lands became known as Red Bones or Brass Ankles depending in which part of the Carolinas they resided. The term Red Bones was the same as saying Redskin or Indian and although they sometimes suggested that they might have Indian blood they always vehemently denied having Negroid blood. Nevertheless the poor treatment which they often received at the hands of the "whites" caused many South Carolina Red Bone families to migrate out of the area. Beginning at the end of the 1700's, many of them left for Alabama and Louisiana. Again during the early 1830's additional Red Bone families journeyed to join their kin in Louisiana where they settled primarily in Rapides Parish and where many of them presently reside, thus the Louisiana Red Bones. The treatment at the hands of the "whites" was no better than they had received in South Carolina thus many of them isolated themselves. The Red Bones of South and North Carolina have traditionally called themselves "malungeans,"[9] and the Red Bones of Louisiana are only now beginning to learn that they, too, are part of that group of isolates called Melungeons which were at one time thought to reside only in upper east Tennessee. No doubt South and North Carolina "Malungeans" (Red Bones and Brass Ankles) also migrated north into upper northwestern North Carolina and eastern Tennessee into that triangle where Tennessee, Virginia, and Kentucky come together. These Melungeons had no better fortune in eastern Tennessee and southwestern Virginia. Their dark complexions mattered not to the Indians, but when the English settlers began to push into that region the old racial prejudices were relighted. By 1834, an estimated three thousand to five thousand Melungeons lived in the region of Newman Ridge in Hancock County, Tennessee. The same upthrust that forms Newman Ridge extends northward into Lee and Wise County, Virginia. During the early 1790's, the Constitutional Convention of Tennessee granted every free man, regardless of color, full citizenship rights, however in 1834 the State of Tennessee limited their rights using the "color barrier" as a de facto way of taking away their right to vote and other rights. Consequently the Melungeons could neither testify against "whites" nor could they bring suit against "whites." Legal problems between Melungeons were held by tribunal rather than court of law. By this single move these dark complexioned people were placed at the total mercy of the "whites." Little by little the Melungeons living in the good bottomland farms yielded their farms to the "whites," unable to defend themselves in court.

Consequently they moved up on the ridges along the eastern rim of the Cumberland Plateau where they fortified and armed themselves in their mountain strongholds. I have heard more than one life-long resident of Hancock County state that not even the sheriff of Hancock County dared to enter their domain. One of the most unfortunate consequences of the 1834 edict was that the children of "persons of color" could not attend the same schools as the "whites." These disenfranchised children of Caucasian origin did not go to school at all since the taxing jurisdictions in many cases failed to provide funds for Melungeon schools. This unfortunate condition existed for many decades until the later part of the 1800's and beginning of the 1900's when Presbyterian Missionaries came into the ridges and hollows to establish schools for Melungeon children. One of the best known Presbyterian Missionary communities was located in Cocke County, Tennessee several miles from Del Rio, Tennessee, high up Caton Chapel Road. It was to this Mission School that Catherine Marshall's mother came to teach. Catherine wrote the prizewinning book *Christy* which dealt with Catherine Marshall's mother's experiences among the people of the Tennessee back country. What is not commonly known except by some people of that region was that the student body was made up of Melungeon children, not Scot-Irish. The Del Rio vicinity has a large Melungeon population although nobody brags about it.

In Wise County, Virginia which also has a very large population of Melungeons, many people of the towns still do not dare venture into the backcountry. Some have expressed amazement that the author has visited those isolated Melungeon communities such as Coeburn Mountain for example, without incident. My own experience among these people has been pleasant and cordial. The Melungeons I have encountered are warm, friendly, hospitable hosts. Of course I do not troupe up there with camera and recorder in hand asking where can I find the Melungeons? What names would one find in the Melungeons communities? As early as 1755 those Melungeon family names enumerated on tax lists included Boulden, Bowlin, Bowling, Bolton, Bunch, Collins, Collens, Colins, Fields, Gibson, Gepson, Goins, Goen, Goan, Goings, Minor, Mullins, Scott.[10] I noted several of these names on mailboxes by the side of the road during my many ventures into the Melungeon communities in Tennessee, Virginia and Kentucky.

The Melungeon Lumbee base differs from the other Melungeon basis primarily because it came from a different group of Spanish pioneers. Whereas the Melungeon/Red Bone/ Brass Ankle isolates are principally descendant from the Juan Pardo (1566) pioneers, the Lumbees draw their heritage from the Lucas Vasquez de Ayllon (1526) colonists and/or shipwrecked Spaniards from the Menendez fleet (1558). The Lumbees although they are oftentimes referred to as Croaton Indians bear little resemblance to the American Indian phenotype. They for the most part bear very close resemblance to the other Melungeon isolates. Additionally like the other isolates, they have traditionally denied Negroid blood, and have kept themselves removed from the blacks. The label Croaton Indian has little bearing on their heritage. In the words of the individual, one Hamilton McMillan of Robeson County, North Carolina: "I gave them the designation of Croaton Indians in the Act. I wanted to give them some designation. There was a tribe known as Croaton tribe on Croaton Island, it was an honorable name and it was a complete designation."[11] Additionally Hamilton McMillan also testified before the Supreme Court of North Carolina in 1915 that those dark complexioned people of Robeson County, North Carolina called themselves Malungeans well before he gave them the designation of Croaton. I might add that nowhere in the 1915 Supreme Court document was the term Lumbee used to apply to those people. The term Lumbee is undoubtedly a much later label and takes cognizance of the fact that these Malungeans reside in large numbers in and about Lumberton, North Carolina on the Lumberton River which is not too far distant from the river, deep in the North Carolina wilderness where Francis Yeardley in 1654 noted that there was a Spaniard residing there having about thirty in family (community).[12] Yeardley also mentions that further to the south and west there is an Indian nation, the Haynokes who valiantly resist the Spaniards' further northern attempts.

Not too long past, the author journeyed to Robeson County. During my trip, I visited the campus of Pembroke State University at Pembroke, North Carolina a mere ten miles northeast of

Lumberton. The faces of many of the students were very familiar to me. They very definitely displayed a western Mediterranean look, i.e. Iberian. During that same trip, I continued north with the thought of revisiting the Suffolk Melungeons. I never reached the Dismal Swamp as I was distracted by a road-sign which read Gaston on the north side of the Roanoke River in the vicinity of Roanoke Rapids, North Carolina. The familiar faces of Melungeons were everywhere to be seen. They, of course scorned the label Melungeons, stating that they were Portuguese, and that their ancestors dated back to the 16th century. Gaston lies sixty miles up the Roanoke River from Ayllon's San Miguel de Guandape. A close examination of a present-day map of that area revealed several Spanish-named backwoods name-places, i.e. Bilboa, Castalia, Liberia, Rhea, Galatia, Palmyra, Menola, Valhalla, Barco, Acre, Aurora, Calico and several other possibilities. A noted author wrote recently that to attempt to impute that any large-scale relationship between the Melungeons and the Lumbees (Malungeans) seems to be merely romantic thinking until something more concrete in the way of evidence turns up.

There is no better evidence than verifiable historical data in the telling of the history of a people. History begins when the first bit of verifiable historical data is brought to light. Oftentimes additional information is needed to complete the historical account of any event or of a people. The Melungeon saga can be told using primarily the written record, however, in order to demonstrate and to further convince, the chronicler needs to draw on places, names and artifacts. A few years ago when I was trying to get my first manuscript published, i.e. *The Spanish Pioneers Along The Atlantic Seaboard*, I was asked by an editor of a university press to tell him why he should recommend publishing my manuscript? It appeared to him that what I had to say in more than five hundred manuscript pages could be told in ten pages or less since it looked to him that it was nothing more than a travel itinerary of Spanish visitors to our eastern shores. He added certainly they had probably been there, but what big cities, what big institutions, what monuments had they left behind? My reply to that young man must have startled him as I fairly exclaimed: "My God man! They left a people. What more could anyone leave? Didn't you read my manuscript?"

He had a point though, I was weak in the names, places, and artifacts department. During the next six years, I hunted high and low for those names, places and things. I found the information which I was seeking in all three categories. The trail from the original Pardo and Ayllon settlements led me west across the Mississippi, up the Missouri to its source and into south central Canada. All along the trail I looked into Melungeon faces, heard their accounts and collected a gallery of photographs of those incredible people who crossed over Cumberland Gap into present-day Kentucky more than two generations before Daniel Boone. The trail also led me to the backwoods of Georgia, Tennessee, North Carolina, Virginia and Kentucky where today lay ruins of old stone forts used by the original Spanish/Portuguese pioneers and their descendants as they moved north and west. I reviewed old and recent anthropological field notes and reports in search of artifacts which would reflect the presence of Spanish/Portuguese pioneers in the interior of the eastern and north central United States, and I found evidence that Spaniards had been to those places and left "things" behind.

IV
THE STONE FORTS

The archaeological literature of the past contains numerous references to stone walls in the southern Appalachian and upper Piedmont areas of Georgia, Tennessee, North Carolina, Alabama, Virginia and Kentucky. However, the paucity of archaeological data available precluded the study of these stone edifices as parts of a related body of phenomena. The lack of data or reluctance to study the stone ruins is perhaps due to the inherent nature of the ancient ruins themselves. In most instances the ruins, especially the stone walls, enclosures and "forts" are situated on ridges or mountain summits and are usually in inaccessible localities. Consequently, they are not promising sites for recovering artifacts or other archaeologically identifiable specimens. Traditionally, local residents referred to these "forts" as "Old Spanish Forts." During second and third decades of the twentieth century, a trend toward removing "things Spanish" from the history of Georgia, Tennessee, North Carolina, South Carolina and Virginia gained widespread acceptance in the writing of the history of the Southeastern United States. The contributions of Spanish pioneers were ignored and essentially written out of historical accounts, with the exception of Florida whose imposing fortress in St. Agustin has to be accepted at face value. Ironically, having written-off the imposing stone ruins as not being of Spanish origins, the researchers were unable to establish the origin nor function of the ruins. During the years 1955 and 1956, Philip E. Smith of Peabody Museum of Harvard University examined more than a dozen stone ruins of "fort" type configurations in Georgia, Tennessee, Alabama, Kentucky and West Virginia. His findings were reported to the Department of Archaeology and Anthropology of the University of Georgia in October, 1956. However, it was not until 1962 that the University of Georgia published Smith's findings and conclusions in a report entitled *Aboriginal Stone Construction in The Southern Piedmont.* What began as a research project into the origins of stone ruins in the Southern Appalachian and Piedmont region concluded in origins of aboriginal (Indian) stone construction in the Southern Piedmont.

The report's conclusion that the stone ruins are aboriginal and ceremonial is highly tentative and speculative. The report states: "It is needless to point out that this interpretation is highly tentative and speculative, and perhaps need not be taken too seriously. Almost certainly it will be modified as more information is obtained, but it seems worthwhile to make some attempt at interpretation, however tenuous, at this time if to provide a jumping-off point for future investigation...It will be obvious by now that one serious flaw in the line of reasoning presented here lies in the assumptions, wholly unfounded at the present, that the various stone constructions described represent a related complex of prehistoric culture, cultural behavior on a contemporary time horizon, or that they indicate a symbolic concept which maintained a cultural tradition over a long period of time and throughout a large spatial area."..."But, even if we gloss over this barrier and work on the assumption that the phenomena are related, we are still almost in the dark as ever as far as getting at the inherent meaning of the structures is concerned. Even if we knew for certain that a certain group of people in a certain period built them, there are still some difficult handicaps in determining just what were the attitudes or concepts or beliefs in the minds of these people which compelled such behavior....The failure to recover artifacts in or near these remains (unless the artifacts found near Mount Carbon, Madison

County, Kentucky and Brown's Mountain, Georgia walls are pertinent to the construction) has been a disappointing stumbling block in our attempts to define them, but at least this failure has to date been consistent. This may in itself be significant, however. It may not be too unreasonable to entertain the belief that conscious efforts were made to prevent the intrusion of the profane objects of everyday life into these places," i.e. ceremonial grounds.[1]

The report finally states: "It has become something of a standing joke among archaeologists to maintain that when a phenomenon cannot be explained in any other way it can always be labeled "ceremonial" and allowed to go at that. This is taking the easy way out, of course, and in many cases, it does represent sloppy or unimaginative thinking. Therefore, we realize that we are leaving ourselves quite vulnerable to attack and criticism on this score when we suggest that, in our opinion, the structures under discussion are ceremonial in nature, or at the very least represent some form of symbolic rather than strictly utilitarian behavior."[2]

The forty-seven page report makes no mention of the 16th and 17th Spanish presence in the interior Southern Appalachian and Piedmont region, even though verifiable historical data places Spanish pioneers (settlers) not only in the general area, but also in very close proximity to numerous stone enclosures particularly the Juan Pardo settlements and forts where artifacts and other archaeological evidence places Spanish pioneers near some of the very stone enclosures examined by Smith.

One stone enclosure which was not examined by Smith during his 1955 and 1956 investigation was the "fort" located near Manchester, Tennessee at the forks of the Duck Rivers. This old stone fort is probably the most imposing of all the stone enclosures, although the stone ruins on Fort Mountain near Chatsworth, Georgia surely rank alongside the old stone fort at Manchester. Smith comments briefly on the Manchester fort stating that while no accurate dimensions are available, it appears very respectable in size, and that all in all it has a rather defensive appearance.[3] He adds that quite possibly it is not related to the stone walls and enclosures described in the body of his paper, *Aboriginal Stone Construction In The Southern Piedmont*. The most compelling reason for his not having examined the Manchester fort was that the private owner was reportedly "unfavorably disposed" to archaeologists, professional or otherwise. Consequently, it was not until 1966 after the State of Tennessee acquired the land from the owner John A. Chumbley that the Manchester fort was examined by a team of archaeologists headed by Alfred K. Guthe, Head of the University of Tennessee Department of Anthropology.

Charles H. Faulkner was a member of the team, and it was he who prepared the official report to the Tennessee Department of Conservation. In 1968, The University of Tennessee Press published *The Old Stone Fort Exploring An Archaeological Mystery* by Charles H. Faulkner. Faulkner concluded that the fort was aboriginal (Woodland Indians) in origin and ceremonial in nature in spite of the fact that no artifacts were found deep in the walls which could be definitely associated with the erection of the wall.[4]

A total of sixteen trenches and fifteen test pits were excavated in the walls and entrance complex. One trench alone was almost sixty feet long. In hopes of determining the age of the wall, seventeen charcoal samples were collected from the wall for radio carbon dating. Of the seventeen charcoal samples collected, thirteen were culled out because of possible contamination or insufficient quantity. The remaining four samples were submitted to Geochron Laboratories Inc., Cambridge, Massachusetts, for radio carbon dating. Only one sample plausibly dated an in situ association with a constructional feature.[5] Unless the burning happened when the wall was under construction these samples probably came in with the fill dirt that was used between the outer portion of the wall and the inner side of the rock walls. See Figure 17.

Consequently, the dates on three of the samples give only the age of the charcoal itself, not when the walls were actually erected. According to Faulkner, only one sample "plausibly" dated an in situ association with a constructual feature.[6] The ages of the charcoal could possibly range from 45 B.C. to as late as 525 A.D. for a maximum total of almost six hundred years. Faulkner would have us believe based on four small charcoals that it took several centuries of concerted and continuous effort by Indians to complete a wall of less than five thousand feet in length and ranging between four to six feet high except at the entranceway where the walls rose to a height of possibly ten to twelve feet.

The author does not wish to imply that the raising of the walls at Manchester was not indeed a prodigious task. However, the suggestion that a primitive people cooperated over a period of almost six centuries in the building of less than five thousand feet of stone wall appears somewhat fanciful especially with the paucity of archaeological data available.

Faulkner states: "An apparent lack of Woodland remains in the area immediately around the Old Stone Fort should not be construed as an additional enigma of this site. A more intensive survey of the area will probably reveal Woodland sites, either buried by river silt or hidden in uncultivated areas. But even if these sites are not close to the Old Stone Fort, there is a logical explanation of where the builders of this enclosure lived."[7]

The logical explanation given for there being no Indian habitation in the environs of Old Stone Fort was that the Indians did not necessarily live close to where they worshiped. Conceivably, the absence of Indians in the area could be the very reason why the builders placed the fortification where it presently stands (more on that later). Faulkner like Smith before him was faced with the prospect of having to make a decision based on almost negligible or zero anthropological data. In both situations the most obviously missing artifact (an object very crucial to archaeological

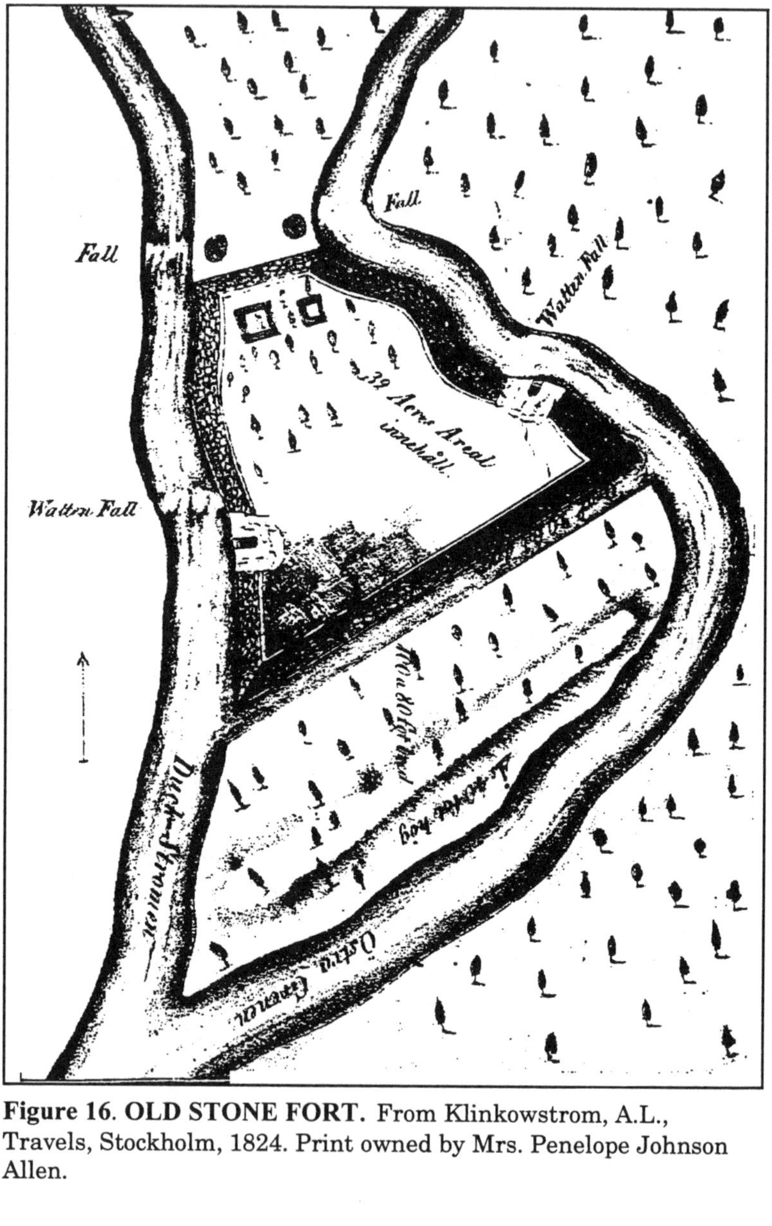

Figure 16. OLD STONE FORT. From Klinkowstrom, A.L., Travels, Stockholm, 1824. Print owned by Mrs. Penelope Johnson Allen.

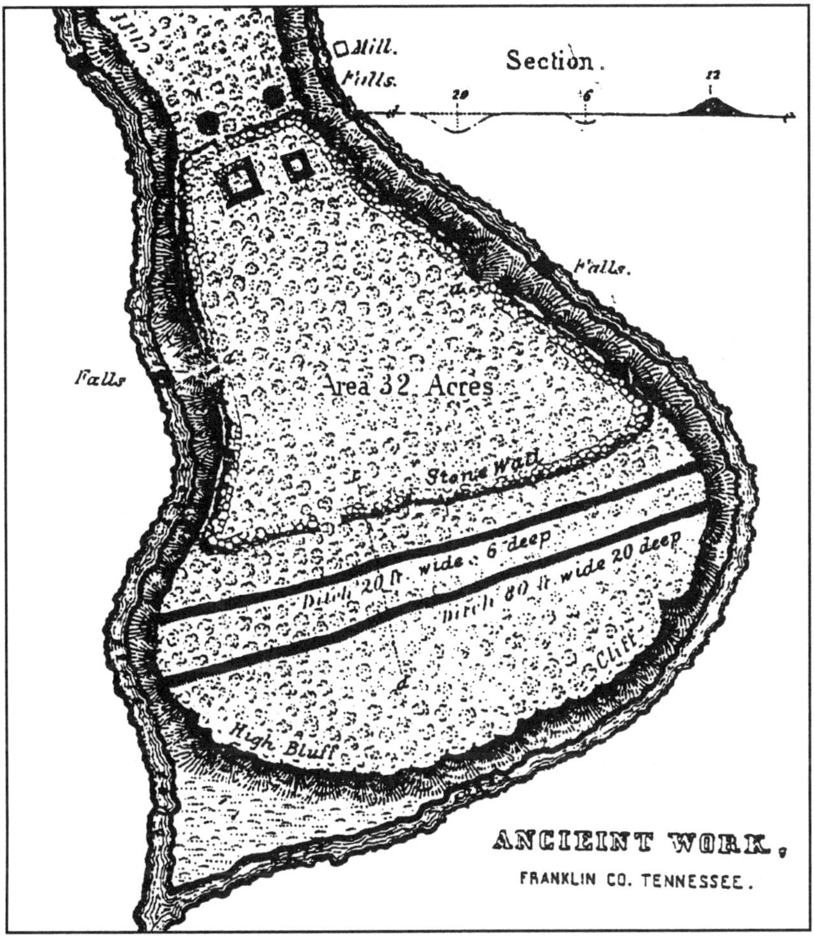

Figure 17. OLD STONE FORT. Squire and Davis, 1848.

excavations) was the lack or total absence of pottery. Faulkner states: "We know that the prehistoric cultures which might have built this enclosure were using pottery by the time the walls were raised, and there are three plausible explanations for its absence in the area. One is that our particular excavation unit just happened to be in areas where sherds were not deposited (i.e. sampling error); the second is that the builders did not use many pottery vessels at this site; third is that the site was carefully cleaned after use. Since the 1966 investigations involved more than twenty large excavation units, the last two possibilities seem more likely than the sampling error. As discussed above in the section on the function of the site, either of these two explanations would support a "ceremonial" theory of the function of the Old Stone Fort."[8]

It is needless to point out that the above "interpretation" is as highly tentative and speculative as Smith's interpretation and like Smith's perhaps should not be taken too seriously. Consequently the standing joke among archaeologists to maintain that when a phenomenon cannot be explained in any other way it can always be labeled "ceremonial" and allowed to go at that was again played on the intellectual community. Although, I might add that Faulkner did not fall into the "unimaginative thinking" category. In the author's opinion, Faulkner's contention that it took almost six centuries of primitive people working cooperatively to build a rock wall less than five thousand feet in length is very imaginative. Particularly when it is based on a single plausible in situ sample of wood charcoal. This plausible in situ sample like the three other charcoal samples as well as the numerous chipped stone artifacts which were recovered probably came in with the fill dirt while the ditches were still open. Faulkner states: "Although aboriginal artifacts were recovered in the walls and in the interior of the enclosure, none of these could be definitely ascribed to the builders of the structure. It is certain that artifacts found deep within the walls or at the bottom of the entrance ditch could be no later than these walls or ditch, but they could indeed be much earlier."[9] Indeed they (the chipped stone artifacts) were much earlier; two items could be Paleo-Indian artifacts, the remainder being either Archaic or Woodland periods. Of the seven projectile points recovered none could be positively associated with Middle Woodland Indians which Faulkner contends were the builders of the Old Stone Fort.

But if the stone enclosures are not ceremonial in nature, the question as to what they are begs for an acceptable answer. Although both Smith and Faulkner argue against the possibility that the stone enclosures are fortifications, every aspect of their nature argues in favor of their purpose being defensive forts. As a rule these forts occur on ridges or mountain summits, usually in rather inaccessible locations, and in most instances a combination of rock walls and the use of natural features of the land such as bluffs, cliffs, steep hillsides which form the defensive enclosure. As in the case of Old Stone Fort in Manchester, Tennessee they were constructed at locations removed from the immediate vicinity of known Indian villages. The nature of their construction and alignment of the entrance-ways and adjacent walls give every appearance of being very defensible, although Smith and Faulkner both insist that from a defensive standpoint they were useless. The author has visited the subject sites more than once, and although the author does not claim to be a military strategist, he has visited numerous, widely acknowledged historic military forts in the Southwestern and Southeastern United States and believes that the forts in question compare very favorably as defensive fortifications. To ignore the defensive aspects of the entrance-way at the Old Stone Fort with its complex features, i.e. high walls, cul-de-sac, high platforms on opposite sides of the main entrance, one must question why such precautions were taken for ceremonial purposes. As stated above, the rock walls comprising the enclosure, exclusive of the strategic entrance-way, were usually between four to six feet high. Both Smith and Faulkner discount the possibility of palisaded walls rising above the rock walls by simply stating that no evidence of palisade posts was found in the fill. Faulkner states: "Since the walls were built at those places on the ridge that lacked the natural protection of the bluffs, it is possible that they were built for defensive purposed. However, two factors cast doubt on this interpretation: the walls are rather low to be an effective barrier, and no evidence of palisade posts was found in the fill. Although organic material would have disappeared rapidly in the clay soil of the area, it seems likely that rotting posts would have left some molds as evidence."[10] The presence of molds of rotting posts in an acid rich soil as is present at Old Stone Fort would not be discernible. During the 1966 excavations, University of Tennessee archaeologists excavated twelve 3x3 test pits and eighty-five mechanically excavated trenches in the enclosed area. Even though a few artifacts and some flint chips were uncovered, no evidence of permanent occupation was discovered. One very important discovery was the absence of a discernible humus line due to the acid content of the soil. A test-trench dug on a site where an old farm house had once stood barely showed a discernible humus line. Anything of an organic composition rapidly turned to soil which explains the reason why no molds of rotted palisade posts were in evidence inside the walls since the acid-rich fill dirt came from borrow ditches inside the enclosed areas as shown in Figure 17 on the following page.

What better way is there to anchor palisade posts in locations where the soil is very shallow as was the case in the other stone enclosures of the Southern Appalachian and Piedmont region? This was especially true of those forts which were located on high mountain ridges such as Alec Mountain, Fort Mountain, Mt. Alto and Sand Mountain all of which were located in close proximity to the Juan Pardo forts and towns.

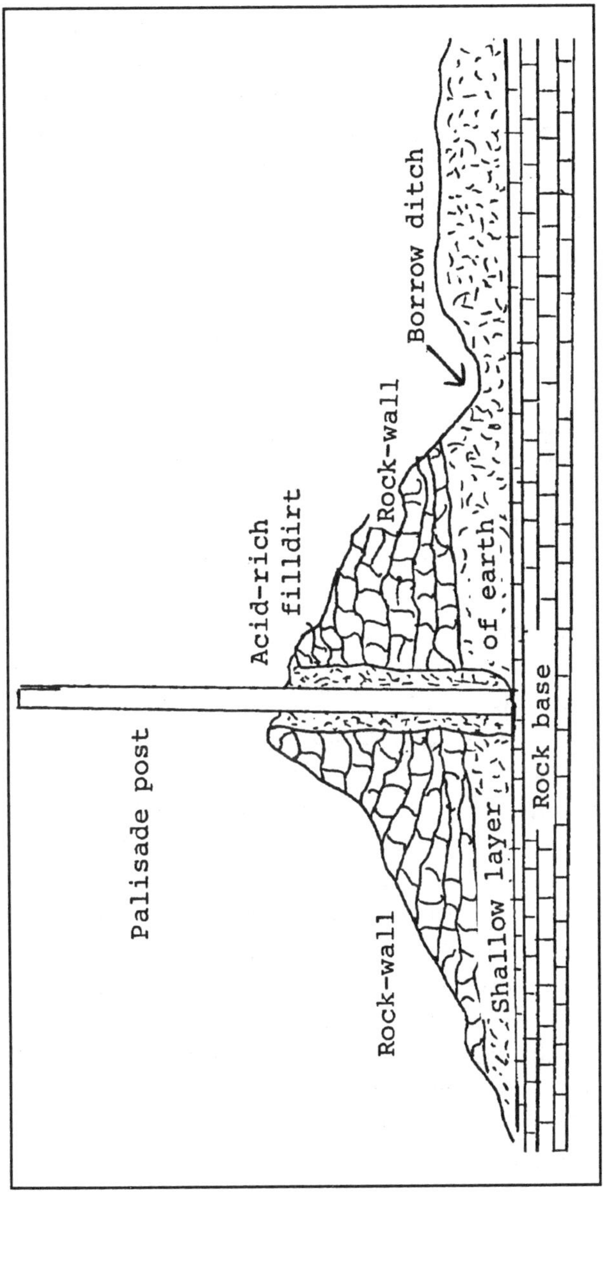

Figure 18. PALISADE POST CROSS SECTION

The above discussion pertaining to the origin and nature of the stone enclosures is based on anthropological and archaeological data. The paucity of reliable information gathered by anthropologists from both the University of Tennessee and Harvard University can hardly be sufficient to conclude (although rather reluctantly) as both Philip E. Smith of the Peabody Museum Harvard University and Charles H. Faulkner of the University of Tennessee that the stone enclosures were ceremonial in nature. Smith does not venture into the question of their age, however, Faulkner places the age of the Old Stone Fort at Manchester at a maximum of 45 B.C. to a minimum of 525 A.D. ± the margin of error associated with radio carbon dating.[11] Faulkner bases his conclusion of age on one (1) plausible in situ, a piece of wood charcoal which like the other artifacts could have been in the general area long before the walls were erected.

By placing the age of the walls between 45 B.C. and 525 A.D., Faulkner eliminated everybody except Indians as the builders of The Old Stone Fort. In recorded history the first non-Indians to arrive as settlers in the Southeastern United States including the Appalachian and Piedmont regions were Spaniards during the 1500's. Lucas Vasquez de Ayllon in 1526 and Juan Pardo in 1566. Both Smith and Faulkner concluded that the forts were not for defensive purposes in as far as the Indians were concerned. This is probably true since although some of the Indians which the Spaniards encountered in the interior did construct defensive fortifications, the fortifications were of the nature of fortified towns which they inhabited. Neither Smith nor Faulkner considered the possibility of non-Indians, i.e. Europeans, being the builders of the stone enclosures. Faulkner added additional emphasis regarding his position on the stone forts of the Southeastern United States in a document which he provided to a newspaper column. On August 13, 1993 Faulkner was quoted as having written to the Knoxville News Sentinel that he (Faulkner) was concerned with the perpetuation of the myth that Europeans (in this case Pardo's men) built the so-called stone forts that dot the Southeast and in particular the forts near Helen and Rome, Georgia and Great Falls, South Carolina. Faulkner is quoted as stating: "Archaeological excavations have been done at several of these and nary a Spanish artifact has ever showed up. There is overwhelming evidence from artifacts and radio carbon dates that they were built by prehistoric Indians, most probably during the Middle Woodland period about 2000 years ago. They are believed to be ceremonial." To what overwhelming evidence from artifacts and carbon dates did Faulkner refer? Faulkner's statements lack veracity. There is no overwhelming evidence of an archaeological nature. Furthermore, the paucity of archaeological evidence as noted above speaks for itself as well as to the lack of intellectual integrity.

ii

The first of the Juan Pardo forts and the nearby Spanish town of Cuenca were situated in the present-day Nacoochee Valley in northern Georgia near the head-waters of the Chattahoochee in the heart of early Cherokee territory or Chalaque as it was called by the Spaniards of the 1540 Hernan de Soto expedition into the interior of the Southeastern United States. Juan Pardo's expedition, like Soto's before him, followed the same ancient Indian land route — the same paths used by animals migrating north-south. Pardo departed from Cofitachequi located on the Savannah River below present-day Augusta, Georgia at Silver Bluff on the South Carolina side of the river sometimes called Spanish Cutoff where C.C. Jones Jr. notes that at Silver Bluff at the Savannah River various monuments and remains of the residence of ancients were visible as late as the 1770's. Such vestiges included conical mounds, terraces, public areas as well as remains or traces of fortresses of regular formation.[12]

After departing from the Cofitachequi vicinity, Pardo followed the high ridge which parallels the river on the South Carolina side as far as its junction with the Tugaloo River. Just below the junction of the two rivers, Pardo forded the Savannah and continued up the left bank of the Tugaloo before turning west toward present-day Clarksville, Georgia passing north of Toccoa. After passing north of Clarksville the Spaniards took a northwesterly direction traveling up the broad, green valley of Beaver Dam Creek almost to its source where they turned west and assaulted the low place along the ridge of present-day Alec Mountain which had long before been the principal crossing of Alec Mountain of the ancient thoroughfare. Once atop the heavily wooded mountain ridge they caught site of a principal Indian town in the broad, green valley below. The town lay nestled beside a small rapid stream (Amos Creek) close under a mountain (Alec Mountain) as described by the chroniclers of both

De Soto and Pardo. De Soto's historians called the Indian town Xuala or Juala (x's and j's in Spanish are often transposed) while the Pardo chroniclers called it Joara or Juada. A general map of the area dated July 27, 1738 by Col. S. Bull, President and Commander in Chief of South Carolina shows Joara and Nacocsee in the vicinity of the present-day Nacoochee Valley.

According to Thomas N. Lumsden, MD., historian of the Nacoochee Valley, Eleazer Early's 1817 map of that part of Georgia shows two Indian towns located within or near the environs of the present-day Nacoochee Valley. The two towns, Chota and Nacocsee are both shown on the map, the former being located in the Nacoochee Valley. The latter is shown situated a short distance to the east, apparently close to the foot of Alec Mountain along the course of a main present day and ancient thoroughfare. The present-day Sautee Creek which flows into the Chattahoochee River at the eastern end of the Nacoochee Valley is shown as Chota River.[13] According to James Mooney, nineteenth century anthropologist, Sautee is derived from Itsati which is a variation of Echota or Chote in Cherokee.

The cacique of the Province of Joara or Juada whose town, lay nestled close under the mountain received Pardo's Spaniards in a friendly fashion and gave them food to eat. The Spaniards rested for a few days at Nacocsee before continuing their journey to Chiaha. However, due to the lateness of the season with snow already covering the high mountain valleys and passes Pardo turned eastward toward Guatari and eventually returned to Santa Elena. Before departing from Juada however, Pardo ordered that a fort be built and left thirty men under the command of Sgt. Bayano with orders to remain and hold the land for Spain. The fort was thus constructed on a relatively level place on the spine of the main ridge of Alec Mountain about one thousand feet north of the road which crosses Alec Mountain at the low place along the spine. The fort was constructed of stones which are found in large quantities laying on the surface all along the long ridge of Alec Mountain, and the stone part was at that time at least six feet high. The north-south outside diameter is approximately one hundred seven feet while the east-west length is ninety-two feet for about nine thousand square feet of about one-fifth acre. The "Spanish Fort" as it was called by the early English settlers until almost recent times was intended to be a place of refuge from impending Indian attack. It was not intended that the Spaniards reside inside the fort since in addition to the fort, Pardo also ordered that a Spanish town also be established to be called Cuenca for its sister city in Spain. The stone fort on Alec Mountain in Habersham County, Georgia was one of the stone ruins studied by Smith of the Peabody Museum, Harvard University in 1956. Although no artifacts were recovered (Indian or Spanish), Smith concluded, and C. Faulkner agreed that the purpose of the structure was ceremonial. Smith in his final report states: "The enclosure is built on a relatively flat area on the spine of the ridge but although a deep gulley lies on one side and (a) fairly steep slope on the other it does not give the impression of being a defensive structure. No documentary evidence had been located to justify the local designation of "Old Spanish Fort."[14]

The author has visited the site and studied the surrounding area numerous times, and finds no justification for Smith's remarks pertaining to the defensibility of the position. Thirty Spaniards armed with guns, crouching behind a six foot stone wall, facing Indians with lances and arrows constitute a formidable defensive posture no matter the lay of the land. As for the lack of documentary evidence, Smith as has Faulkner ignored the presence of Pardo and his soldier/settlers in that exact part of present-day Georgia for which there are at least four Spanish documents written by writers that were contemporaries to the events of 1566 and 1567 in the interior of the Southeastern United States.

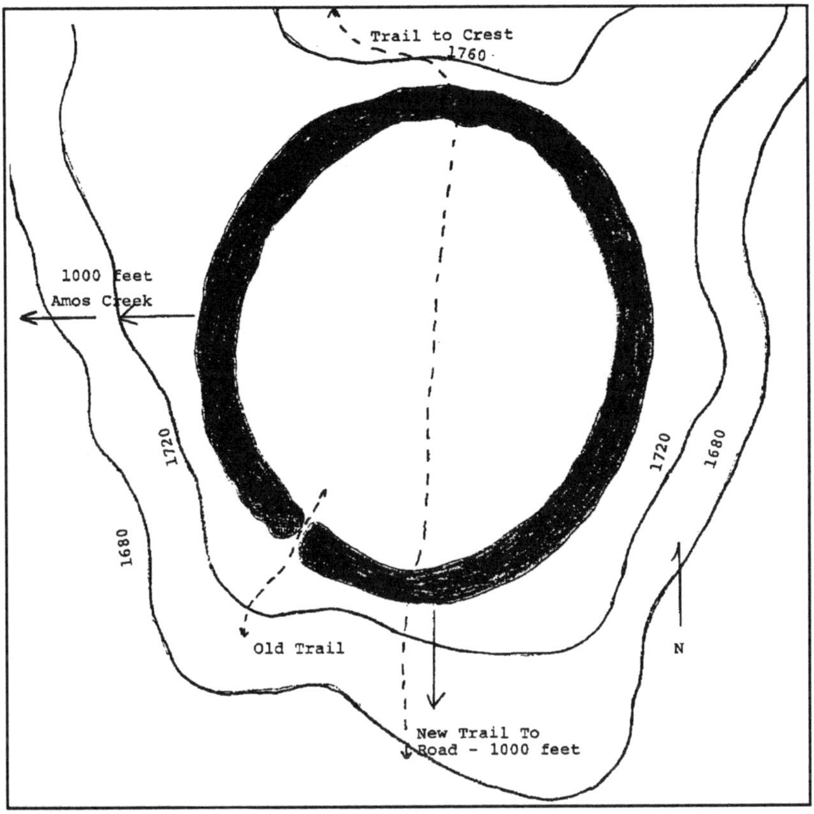

Figure 19. FORT SAN JAUN DE JUADA
ALEC MOUNTAIN, HABERSHAM COUNTY, GA.

Below the ridge toward the west looking down into the lush, green valley with a swift stream meandering between the Indian habitations, the first Spaniards viewed the Indian town of Juada with its fortified town quadrangle. The author recently stood on that very spot where the first Spaniards stood. Like them I, too, viewed the valley with the swift stream, Amos Creek, flowing southward where a short distance its waters merged with the much larger Chattahoochee. On descending into the valley, I visited with John Arnold of the Amy's Creek community who informed me that as recently as twenty years ago when he was still plowing his fields, large numbers of pottery sherds could be viewed. In addition he pointed out two mound-like features in the center of the valley which appeared unnatural as part of the geography of the land. These two rather large mounds in all probability are of the same genre as another mound-like structure a short distance away in the center of the Nacoochee Valley. The mound in the Nacoochee Valley has been determined to be of Indian origins and is very prominent on the valley floor.

Spanish artifacts of the 1500's have been recovered and reported in the Nacoochee Valley as early as the 1830's.[15] One such artifact was a pair of silver cigar tongs ascribed to Spanish occupancy. But more significant than the silver cigar tongs or sherds was the discovery of a subterranean village in the vicinity of the Spanish fort of San Juan de Juada. In 1873, C.C. Jones in his *Antiquities of The Southern Indians* wrote the following: "In 1834, Colonels Merriwether and Lumsden, while engaged in digging a canal in Dukes's Creek Valley for the purpose of facilitating their mining operations, unearthed a subterranean village consisting of thirty-four small cabins, located in a straight line extending upward of three hundred feet. They were made of logs hewn at the ends and notched down, after the fashion of the rude log-huts of the present day. This hewing and notching had evidently been done with sharp metallic tools, the marks being such as would have been caused by a chopping axe. Above these little houses-situated from fifty to one hundred yards from the principal channel of the creek, and embedded from seven to nine feet below the surface of the ground — trees were growing from two to three feet in diameter. The estimated age of these trees was somewhat over two hundred years. The violent changes often caused, in their narrow valleys and along their yielding banks by mountain streams swollen with rain or engorged by the dissolving snows of winter, may account for the inhumation of these cabins within a comparatively short period after their abandonment."[16]

Dukes Creek enters the Chattahoochee almost at the center of the Nacoochee Valley where the early Cherokee village of Chota was situated. Also in close proximity of Dukes Creek, but on the eastern end of the Nacoochee Valley another prominent water course enters the Chattahoochee. Thomas N. Lumsden, M.D., in his excellent book, *Nacoochee Valley Its Times And Its Places*, points out that in addition to the subterranean cabins along Dukes Creek with its hand hewn logs, remains of mid-sixteenth century evidence of European occupancy was discovered in 1834.[17] Bean Creek's deep auriferous gravels yielded hewn pitch pine which came from Childs Mine on lot 23 on Bean Creek. Childs Mine was located west of the Spanish Fort on Alec Mountain and northeast of the sixteenth century Spanish town of Cuenca located on Dukes Creek. Both James Mooney and C.C. Jones Jr. share the opinion that Spaniards of the sixteenth century came into the Nacoochee Valley. More recently, Hudson, Halley and DePratter disagree with Mooney and C.C. Jones, however, in the author's opinion although Hudson and company claim to have new data on De Soto's and Pardo's routes, no new data was introduced pertaining to the route itself. Consequently, this author most emphatically rejects Hudson and company's conclusion that neither De Soto nor Pardo entered the Nacoochee Valley.

The next fort in Pardo's line-of-travel was located over the mountains toward the west and north. After leaving the Nacoochee Valley, the Spaniards of Pardo's expedition of settlement proceeded along the ancient Choestoe Trail up Dukes Creek until its junction with present-day Dodd Creek to its source below Wildcat Mountain where they climbed to the top of the ridge and Hogpen Gap. From the Gap one can look toward the northeast a few miles and view Spaniard's Knob and Spaniard Mountain named for the first settlers of those interior lands. At a later date Pardo's soldier/settlers would move north out of the Nacoochee Valley up the Unicoi Trail to the Hiwassee River which ran along the eastern base of Spaniard Mountain. On descending from Hogpen Gap toward the north, the party of Spaniards arrived at the upper reaches of the Nottely River whose valley they followed to present-day Blairsville, Georgia where they turned west along the high mountain ridge which led to the Indian town of Tocax lying along the banks of the Toccoa River near present-day Blue Ridge, Georgia. From Blue Ridge, the Spaniards took the direction of southwest and after a short march reached Cherry Log Creek which they followed to its junction with the Ellijay River. The route from Blue Ridge to Ellijay, Georgia was probably very close to the route of the Louisville and Nashville Railroad. From Ellijay, Pardo and his men followed the Indian path which connected the lower overhill Cherokee towns to the more eastern Cherokee towns of the Nacoochee Valley (Juada/Xuala). The path lay northwest out of Ellijay along present-day State Road 52 to the old Indian town of Mountaintown about twelve miles distant where they temporarily headed north along the broad, green valley of Mountaintown Creek which they followed almost to its source before turning west along Barnes Creek. Pardo and his men followed Barnes Creek a short distance to its source on the eastern side of Holly Creek Gap which sits at about two thousand feet above sea level and four hundred feet higher than the valley below.

Below Holly Creek Gap towards the west, the high mountain creek of the same name breaks from between high mountain ridges into a broad, lush, green valley. Again the Spaniards followed the Indian trail leading westward toward the lower overhill Cherokee towns. The first major town which they encountered was De Soto's Conasauga which Pardo and his chroniclers called Cauchi or Cohutta which lay along the banks of Holly Creek in the wide valley between present-day Chatsworth, Georgia on the west and Fort Mountain on the east (2800 feet above sea level) which rises more than 2000 feet straight up from the valley floor. Holly Creek goes on to join with the Conasauga River a short distance west of Chatsworth. Cohutta Mountain, from which the Indian town derived its name, rises to about 2700 feet above sea level and is a little more than two miles due south of Fort Mountain. During an early April 1997 visit to the Fort Mountain and Holly Creek environs, the author located an individual who was familiar with the Cherokee language. The author asked this individual to pronounce "Cohutta" in the Cherokee idiom. Accordingly the individual pronounced "Cohutta" as "Co hoo cha" rather than "Co hoo ta" explaining that double "tt's" were often given the guttural sound of "cha." Pardo and his chroniclers hearing it pronounced thus used the phonetic sound spelling as "Cauchi." But why then did De Soto's chroniclers call this same Indian town, Conasauga? Pardo's chroniclers also mentioned the name Conasauga in their *relaciones* but only in reference to an Indian caciquess named Conasauga who had ruled in that part of Indian lands for a long time. Often times Spanish visitors to Indian towns attached the name of the cacique or caciquess of the particular town to the town itself. Apparently this ancient caciquess, Conasauga, of De Soto's time (1540) also came to meet with Pardo in the middle 1560's. One of Pardo's chroniclers, Vandera, relates that during the Caciquess Conasauga's visit to Cauchi, Pardo presented her with a very generous presentation of gifts.

Pardo had been ordered by Menendez de Aviles to build a strong fort at Cauchi. However, before doing so, Pardo was to visit another principal Indian town toward the south and west the Coosa (Creek) town of Chiaha where he had also been ordered to build a strong fort and hold the land for His Majesty Felipe II as a point along the overland route from the Gulf of Mexico to the Atlantic Ocean. Consequently after a short stay at Cauchi, Pardo and his men proceeded south and west. This time they followed the Conasauga River until it joined with the Coosawatti River entering from the northeast to form the Oostanaula River which they followed southerly to present-day Rome, Georgia where the Oostanaula joined with the Etowah to form the Coosa River. Chiaha, the famed principal Indian town of De Soto, Tristan de Luna and Pardo lay on the peninsula formed by the twisting, turning Etowah and Oostanaula Rivers as they finally joined their waters after meandering in the lush, broad meadows on which present-day Rome, Georgia sits. The bottomlands of the twisting, winding rivers of that day were much lower than the land on which Rome, Georgia sits today and in at least two places the rivers almost touched at very narrow necks. Undoubtedly during high water times, the rivers joined temporarily at the low narrow necks creating large islands as the Spanish chroniclers have related. De Soto was the first European to pass through this part of the Southeastern United States. The second group of Spaniards to venture into northeastern Georgia was an advance party sent by Tristan de Luna in 1559 to scout the road from present-day Pensacola, Florida to the farthest Coca (Coosa) principal town, i.e. Chiaha. The chronicler of this expedition reported the vast meadows and near-islands in addition to the Indian huts perched on a high hill outside the Indian village. This high hill could very well be present-day Myrtle Hill immediately west of the Etowah River just before it joins the Oostanaula River in downtown Rome, Georgia. While at Chiaha, the leader of the advance party inquired about a certain soldier which De Soto feared would certainly die if he continued on the march. Consequently Soto decided to leave the ill soldier behind at Chiaha believing that he would die very shortly thereafter. The Spaniards were informed that although the soldier in question was no longer alive he had lived for many years after being left behind by Soto. The soldier had married an Indian woman and until his death two years prior had been an accepted member of the Indian community.

So when Pardo came among the Coosas in 1566, he was the third European to venture into the principal Indian town of Chiaha. Since the Coosas had experienced nothing but favorable relations with the Spanish, the cacique offered Pardo the use of Indian labor for building a proper fort and requested in return that Pardo leave men behind to teach the Indians about the Spaniard's God. The most defensible location for a fort was located about three and one-half miles toward the southwest atop Mt. Alto (High Mountain) on present-day Horseleg Mountain. What could be the remains of that fort are visible today in the form of two stone walls which extend along the highest part of the ridge which forms the mountain.[18] One of these walls is composed of irregularly shaped stones roughly stacked several feet high. The wall ruins run in a north-south direction along the ridge for about one hundred fifty feet, and although the wall was probably longer when it was originally built, its exact length cannot be determined since much of it has been removed for construction purposes. The other wall or what remains of it is situated about one hundred feet south to the former, and it too runs north-south parallel with the spine of the ridge but on the west side. Its present visible length is about seventy-three feet. Quite possibly the two walls might at one time have been one continuous wall isolating the highest part of Mt. Alto from intruders.

Pardo named the fort, Fort San Pedro and departed from Chiaha, leaving behind one clergy and thirty men to man and hold the land for King and Country. Chiaha was strategically situated about half-way along the overland route from Ichuse, present-day Pensacola, and Santa Elena, present-day Beaufort, South Carolina. After departing from Chiaha, Pardo and party retraced their steps back to Cohutta (Cauchi) where they rested for a few days and in the meantime commenced building the third of four forts deep in the interior. By the time Pardo departed, the fort was almost completed, and it was a small affair capable of being defended if necessary by twelve men. This small affair was probably the first of three fortifications in the Cauchi/Fort Mountain environs, since the nine hundred twenty-five foot wall near the top of Fort Mountain would have exceeded not only the small Spanish contingent's capabilities but also their needs. According to Philip E. Smith of the Peabody Museum of Archaeology and Ethnology, Harvard University during his study of the "stone ruins" in the Southeastern United States he interviewed one James Chambers of Chatsworth, Georgia. Mr. Chambers informed Smith that about thirty years ago he had viewed a well-preserved semicircular horse-shoe shaped stone wall at the base of the cliffs on the west side of the summit, somewhere along the road which leads to the talc mine beneath the Fort Mountain peak. According to Mr. Chambers the wall was about one hundred twenty to one hundred fifty feet around and backed up into the mountain to some sort of cave. The wall ranged in height from one to six feet.[19] The wall was due east about two and one quarter miles from the center of the broad valley of Holly Creek. The talc mine as well as the road is shown on U.S. Geological Survey Maps. During a recent visit to the Fort Mountain area, the author traveled the pertinent road to the talc mine and noted that there were several places where one could back up to the cliffs on the west side into a defensive position.

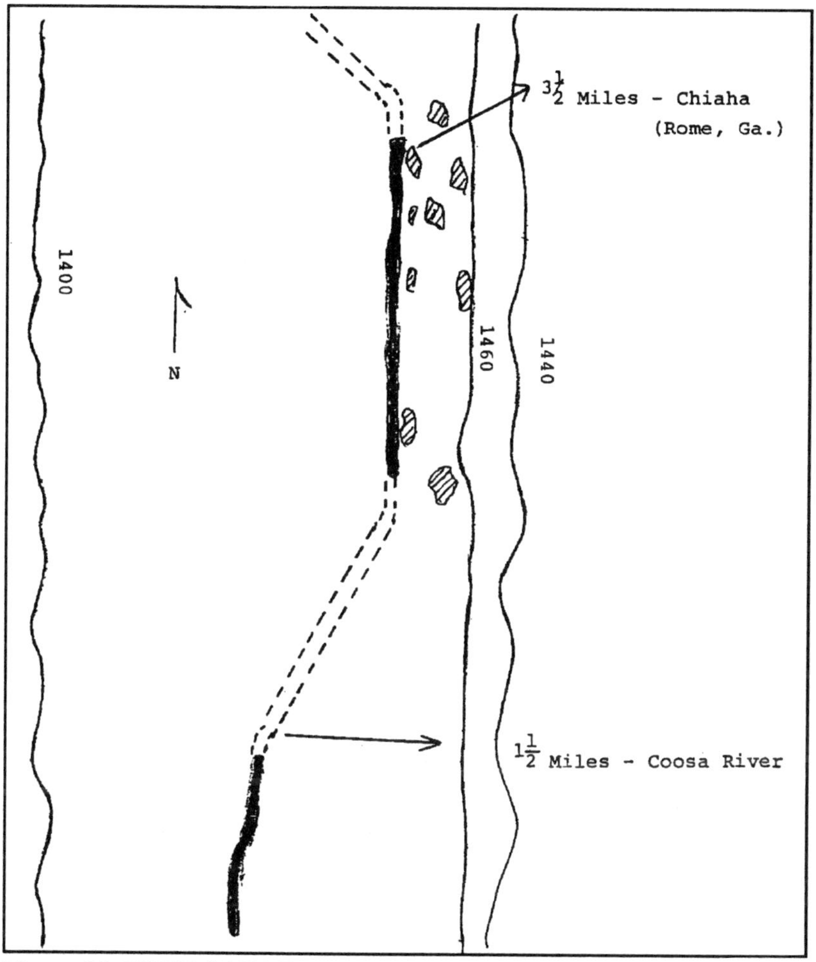

Figure 20. FORT SAN PEDRO—MT. ALTO, ROME, GEORGIA

Smith also states that Mr. Chambers informed him that one Colonel King had also examined the wall and reported his findings to one of the Atlanta Newspapers (approx. 1925). Smith conducted a cursory search of some Atlanta newspaper files but was unsuccessful in his search. Mr. Chambers felt certain that he could locate the wall on foot, but could not detect it from an aerial photograph and was unable to give oral directions to the exact spot. According to Smith he was unable to coax Mr. Chambers to lead him to the site due to Mr. Chambers' age and reluctance to risk the heat and serpents, although Mr. Chambers seemed willing to act as guide during cold weather. The present author can certainly sympathize with Mr. Chambers regarding the heat and snakes, not to mention the age factor. During the author's visit to the talc mine he ,too, did not dare nor wish to venture along too far off the road. In conclusion, Smith notes that Mr. Chambers' account of the walls seemed quite reliable.[20]

A structure of that size would have been very adequate for defensive purposes for so small a number of men, and it was not until a later time when the contingent of Spanish soldier/settlers and their families departed from Chiaha to join their fellow countrymen at Cauchi that a larger more commodious fort was required. Even during the time when Pardo was at Chiaha, the safety of the men remaining behind was not guaranteed since the Indian nations toward the west of Chiaha beyond the Appalachian Mountains posed a threat to the Spaniards and the Coosas at Chiaha. Consequently at some later date the Spaniards at Chiaha journeyed northward to Cauchi seeking safety in numbers, and it was probably at that time that the fort atop the promontory later called Fort Mountain was begun. It appears that between the time that the Spaniards abandoned their first fort at the western foot of the promontory and occupied the fort near the top of the mountain, they built an intermediate fort about one thousand feet below the top of the mountain at about one thousand seven hundred feet above sea level. As late as 1955 the walls of this intermediate stone enclosure were visible. According to Smith in his final report, these ruins could be reached by a logging road leading up the back side of Fort Mountain from Hassler Mill and Cool Spring at a distance of about two miles. The ruins consisted of rough stones piled a few feet and formed a rough enclosure. The stones appeared to have been taken from a heavy rock-fall in the vicinity.

At this point, The Spaniards were less than one-half mile from the present-day Fort Mountain stone ruins. During April of 1997, the author visited the place where the logging road terminates and although it ends within one-half mile of the Fort Mountain stone fort, the incline is so steep at that place that it would be almost impossible to ascend to the top from there. Instead of climbing up the face of the backside of the mountain I walked about fifteen hundred feet due south along the side of the slope until I intercepted the upper reaches of Mill Creek at about one thousand seven hundred fifty feet above sea level where I turned due west and followed the course of the creek, and although it was steep, I was able to negotiate the climb to a place where the water seeps out of the rock to form a shallow, clear stream which tumbles down the mountain. The place where the water seeped from the rocks was about four hundred feet from the stone wall at a point about two thousand seven hundred fifty feet above sea level and at the very place along the wall where it jogs outward for about fifty-five feet. Alongside the jog toward the east is a break in the wall and where the walls run parallel forming a hallway-like entrance.

At the present time the wall consists of a line of stones running across the slope at approximately the two thousand seven hundred fifty foot contour line. This contour line runs along a low place or saddle which separates the top of Fort Mountain on the north from the lower ridges and peaks to the south. The wall itself is approximately nine hundred feet long, and at each end the slope of the mountain drops precipitously. It is composed of stone taken from the immediate area. The size of the stones vary from small ones weighing a few pounds to extremely large boulders of several tons. The average height of the wall is between three to four feet, although in several places it reaches the height of ten feet. It varies in width from sixteen feet to a minimum of four and one-half feet which raises the possibility that at the places where it is sixteen feet wide it could have been much higher since the stones could have tumbled down making the base much wider at those places. Although presently there is no permanent water source within the enclosure, it is entirely possible that at the time that the fort was in use by its original occupants, a source of water existed. The unexplained jog lies along a slight draw which leads to the upper reaches of Mill Creek. It is very possible that the upper reaches of Mill Creek extended farther up the slope to the two thousand seven hundred foot contour line, plus in which case, the jog in the line of stones was used to protect the water source. During my April 1997 visit to the area, a very heavy thunderstorm occurred while I was on the mountain, and I observed water running down the draw which in normal times is a dry water course.

On walking up to the stone wall from the parking area and from the upper reaches of Mill Creek along the draw, one is immediately struck by its strategic location near the relatively narrow saddle which connects the lower ridges to the larger mass of mountain and the summit of Fort Mountain. Located as it is, the stone fortification blocks the passage across the saddle to the higher land behind the wall. Although its present-day height averages between three to four feet, judging from its present width at the base it probably stood somewhat higher at the time of occupation — probably five feet at a minimum. Even though there is no evidence at hand to indicate that at one time its finished height might have been made higher by using logs or branches, one should not conclude that it was not. Any logs or branches would have long decomposed due to exposure for almost four hundred years.

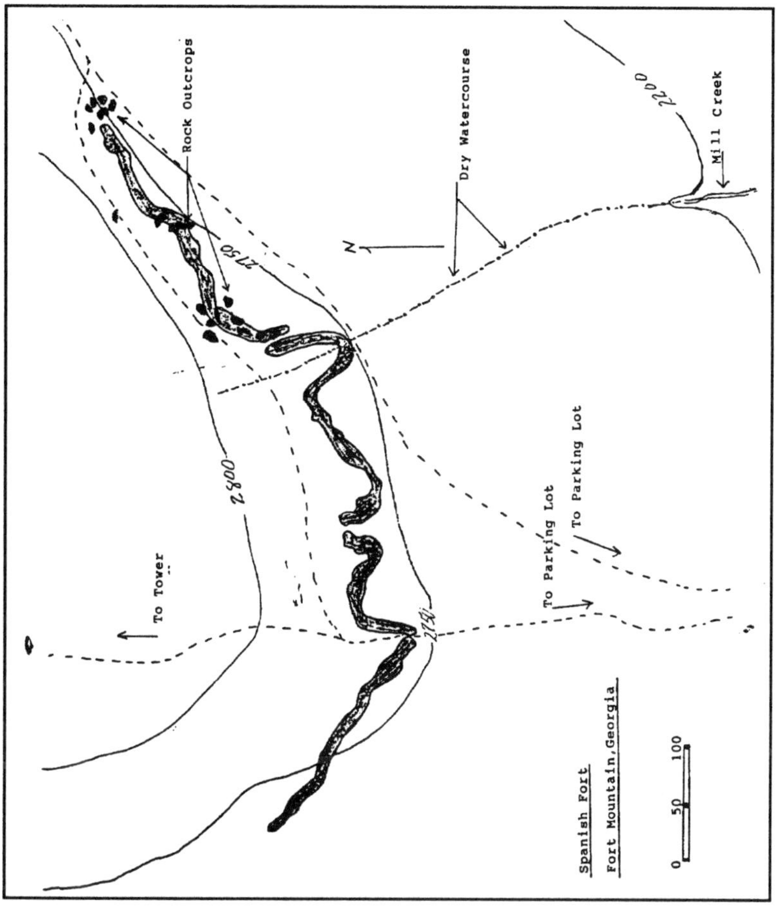

Figure 21. FORT SAN PABLO—CAUCHI

Exposure and thinness of soil could also explain why no archaeological artifacts other than a few projectile points have been recovered. Any perishable refuse would quickly disappear due to exposure and very shallow soil, and it is very unlikely that artifacts would have been preserved by chance burial. Regarding the few projectile points that have occasionally been found within the enclosure, it does not necessarily mean that they were shot in battle. An occasional hunter venturing atop the high promontory could have sent an errant arrow or spear at a fleeing animal.

It is also entirely possible that during the period of time that the Spaniards occupied the fort, they never had the need to crouch behind the stone wall awaiting imminent attack. The Indians at Cauchi were probably Creeks since it was not until later that the Creeks yielded their northernmost lands to the Cherokees who at the time the Spaniards first entered into Cherokee lands, they too were recent arrivals coming in from the east by way of Virginia. The Spaniards had in the past experienced warm relations with the Creeks and Cherokees, a relationship which lasted several generations until the English arrived on the scene. The Chiscas or Yuchis who were at that time occupying lands in East Tennessee in the Tennessee Valley north of the Hiwassee River were the sworn enemies of the Spaniards beginning with De Soto and extending into Pardo's time. Pardo's men under Sgt. Bayano journeyed north to make war with a Chisca cacique who had made dire threats upon the few Spaniards left behind at Fort San Juan de Juada during 1566-67. Sgt. Bayano and his small body of troops soundly defeated the Chiscas, and this action could have made the Chiscas wary of the Spaniards ability and might in making war. Subsequently the Spaniards and their families lived in relative safety from the Indians of that part of northern Georgia and East Tennessee until the day when most of the Spaniards, the predecessors of the Melungeons were forced to move westward. More on that later.

According Mooney who lived among the Cherokees, whom he studied for many years, there has been persistent oral history among the Indians that a strange white race preceded the Cherokee. Some of the accounts go so far as to locate their former settlements and to identify them as the builders of the ancient works found in the country.[21] As early as 1797, Barton in his *New Views* states that the "Ceerake" oral history tells that when they (The Cherokee) first arrived in the Creek country which they the Cherokee presently (1797) inhabited, they found it occupied by certain "moon-eyed people." The oral history goes on to say that they killed some of them, married some of them and expelled some of them. Twenty-six years later in 1823 Haywood in his *Natural and Aboriginal History of Tennessee* says that when the Cherokees first invaded the lands previously occupied by the northern band of Creeks they found "white people" near the head of the Little Tennessee River, with forts extending thence down the Tennessee as far as Chicamauga Creek. Haywood gives the location of the forts as being at the mouth of Chicamauga, Pumpkinton, Fox Taylor's reserve near Hamilton Courthouse, and at Big Chicamauga about twenty miles above its mouth[22] which would place it in the vicinity of the Sand Mountain stone fort in Catoosa County, Georgia. The Pumpkinton fort would have been located close to later day Fort Loudoun in Monroe County, Tennessee. The fort at the mouth of North Chicamauga would have been in the vicinity of present-day Chicamauga Dam near downtown Chattanooga, Tennessee.

The Cherokees made war against the "white people" living in these forts and drove them to the mouth of Big Chicamauga Creek (South Chicamauga Creek), where they entered into a treaty and the "whites" agreed to remove themselves if permitted to depart in peace. The Cherokees agreed and the 'whites' (Spanish/ Melungeons) abandoned the country and headed west. The houses in which these people resided were described by Barton as having been small, circular structures of upright logs covered with earth which had been dug out from the inside. Subsequently, the tradition of "white Indians" has persisted in both Middle Tennessee and Kentucky since the seventeenth century (1600's). Chief Aoonosta of the Cherokees reportedly informed John Sevier (Juan Javier), the first governor of the State of what would later be Tennessee that according to oral history of the Cherokees, his father's fathers often spoke of "whites" in the west in the great hunting grounds. The great hunting grounds in those days were Middle Tennessee and Kentucky. This oral tradition concerning the whites was current at the time (1770's) that Sevier was warring against them. Sevier himself spoke of seeing these non-Indian dark complexioned people with European features. According to the oral history of the Cherokees there had occurred serious clashes between the whites and Cherokees. The final outcome being that the whites were defeated and agreed to leave the Cherokee lands. Some reportedly journeyed to and settled in the Missouri River Country among the Mandan.

On departing from Cauchi, Pardo named the fort, Fort San Pablo and left behind a catechist as requested by the cacique and twelve men to hold the land. His destination was San Juan de Juada and since the fort on Alec Mountain had been built the previous year, Pardo rested for a few days before departing for Guatari where he would erect the fourth fort in the deep interior of the Southeastern United States. However, before departing from San Juan de Juada, he selected thirty-one men and had them remain and hold the land. From San Juan de Juada, Pardo and his remaining men struck due east, however, instead of backtracking down the Unicoi Trail, they headed up the Coosa-to-Tugaloo Trail up the Sautee Valley passing south of present-day Clayton, Georgia and struck another well-traveled trail along upper South Carolina crossing all the major rivers at their low fords. In less than a week Pardo arrived at Catawba country south of present-day Rock Hill, South Carolina where he was well received. As at the other Indian towns, the cacique asked Captain Pardo to leave religious ones to instruct them. The Spaniards built their fourth fort, but unlike the other forts which were constructed of stone, the fort at Guatari was of raised earth and wood. At each corner stood tall cavaliers constructed of thick wood. Between the cavaliers ran a high wall of poles and dirt. Lucas de Canizares was left in command of Fort Santiago and ordered to establish a settlement to be named Salamanca for the city in their native Espana. With Canizares there remained sixteen soldier/settlers and a clergyman, one Father Sebastian Montero. The Spaniards swore before God that they would remain in the interior and hold the land for God and King.

The earth and wood used to construct Fort Santiago unlike the stones used at the other Pardo forts did not survive the passage of time nor the elements into the present day. However at least two writers who have conducted historical research in that part of South Carolina have noted the Spanish presence in or about the Rock Hill, South Carolina country. Wallace M. Reinhardt writes pertaining to earth structures of the country: "We will next notice mounds of the country. Cultivation has now nearly obliterated them though a few can yet be seen, but of the date of the early settlers (1740) they were quite numerous and excited great curiousity.... One old settler believed that they were remains of Indian mud huts which crombled with age and thus accounted for the loose soil upon them. Another thought they were gigantic ant hills built one upon the crumbling ruins of the others. Others believed the mounds to be evidences of ancient fortifications... Even at that remote date the pioneers said some of these mounds were grown up with large trees."[23] Reinhardt, whose manuscript is on file at the Smithsonian Institute also gives detailed descriptions of evidence of early mining in that part of the country before the English arrived.

Another writer, Douglas Summers Brown, in the book, *The Catawba Indians: The People of the River* states: "During my nine-year residence in York County (South Carolina), I heard many tales about the supposed presence of Spanish in that area including one about a "Spanish graveyard" west of Rock Hill. There is also a Calabash, a word probably of Spanish origin, Creek near Clover which bore that name before the coming of the English."[24] Brown also goes on to comment regarding Spanish coins being found buried thirty feet below the surface by well diggers in neighboring Lancaster County. Brown was correct in supposing that "Calabash" had Spanish origins. The correct spelling, however, is "calabasa" meaning pumpkin, squash or gourd. Calabash Creek does not stand alone in that region dominated by English name-places and towns. In that country of northern South Carolina and southern North Carolina between eighty and eighty-one degrees longitude and thirty-four to thirty-six degrees latitude, the names of present-day Spanish name-places and towns are legion. To mention but a few as follows: Saluda, Santo, Sedalia, Seneca, Una, Mayo, Casar, Celo, Valdese, Toluca, Cordova, Eldorado, Cid, Alma, Lando, Angelus, Vandera, Angelico and many other too numerous to list.

The Catawba Indians like their neighbors toward the west, the Cherokee Indians, have traditionally been farther advanced in their standard of living and government than their neighbors. These two peoples were the most open and friendly to the newcomers of European origins. Mooney, in his *Historical Sketch of The Cherokees* speculates on this very point by noting: "How much permanent impression the early Spanish intercourse made on the Cherokee is impossible to estimate, but it must have been considerable."[25] As indeed it was with the Catawbas and to some degree with the upper Creeks. When the myth that the English were always right and the Spanish were always wrong finally crumbles and the intrepid Spanish pioneers become recognized as having had a very significant part in building what is today the United States of America, then and only then will we have a truly comprehensive history of our great country.

V
THE PIONEERS

SPANISH/PORTUGUESE BASE

MELUNGEONS	**RED BONES**	**TURKS**	**BRASS ANKLES**	**LUMBEES**
Tennessee	South Car.	South Car.	South Car.	North Car.
Virginia	Louisiana	North Car.		
Alabama				
Kentucky				
Georgia				
West Virginia				
Arkansas				

Historical accounts and archaeological finds have placed Spaniards in widely separated locations in the Southeastern United States removed from the original places where the Pardo forts were situated. The general migration of the Spaniards and their families took them in a westerly and northwesterly direction into the areas where they reside at the present day. See the following page for the general migration routes. Although many departed from the original sites beginning during the very early years of the 1600's, some remained in the vicinity of the original Spanish forts but removed themselves into the remote back country where they continued to live in isolation. These included the Lumbees, Brass Ankles, Turks and Red Bones of northern South Carolina and southern North Carolina, although many Red Bones removed themselves to the

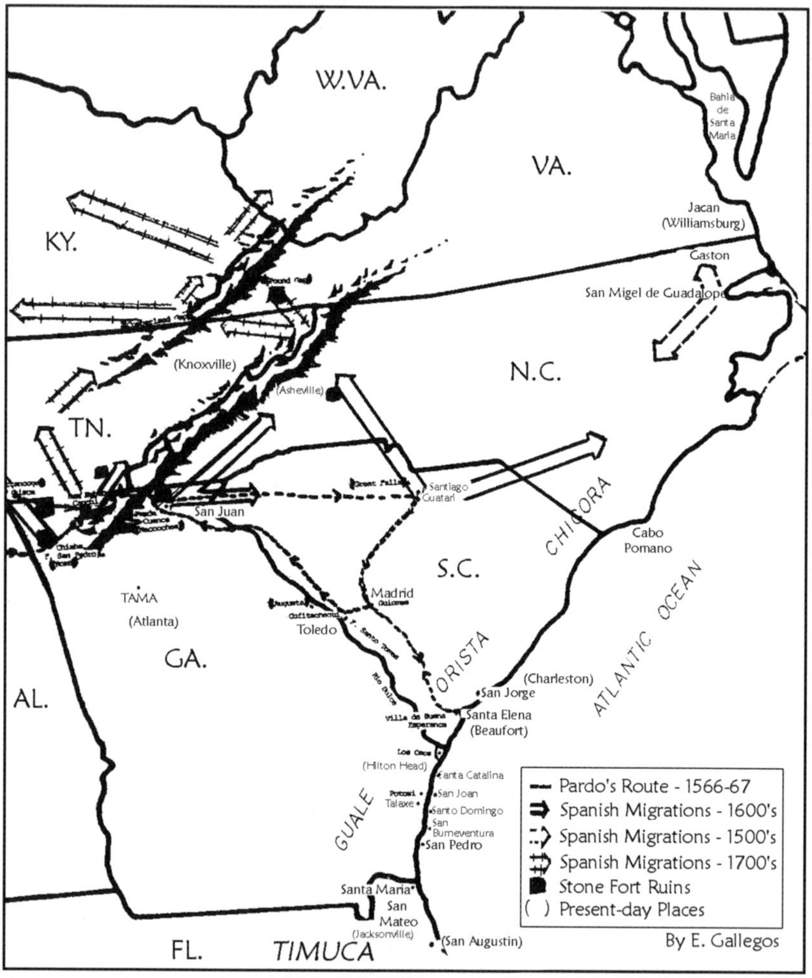

Figure 23. SPANISH MIGRATIONS

Sabine River country of Louisiana where they also lived isolated from the general populace. The Melungeons with but few exceptions did not remain in the original fort country, but tended to spread into the neighboring states; some migrated into the Missouri River country and north thereof. Those in the Southeastern United States tended to reside isolated from their non-Melungeon neighbors — the English settlers moving westward from the Atlantic Seaboard and Piedmont regions over the high mountains of the Appalachian chain. The English settlers being granted large grants of land by their King were much amazed that the free lands toward the west were already occupied by other peoples of European origins, i.e. the descendants of the Spanish/Portuguese soldier/settlers of the Pardo venture. As the number of English settlers grew greater and greater, the isolates were pushed off of their farms and land holdings with no legal recourse as Melungeons were not allowed to testify against a non-Melungeon in a court of law. It soon became clear to the isolates that the only lands which they would be able to hold were those lands which nobody desired — the high ridges and deep hollows of the Cumberland Plateau or the dark swamps of the Virginia-North Carolina tidewater country.

The migrations west and north did not occur during a short period of time. Two or three generations might live in the same locale before moving on. In many cases they took the name of their previous town or village with them. The back roads of all the southeastern states including Alabama, Arkansas, Missouri, Kentucky, West Virginia and, yes, even Ohio, Illinois and Indiana are marked by towns and name-places of Spanish origin too numerous to list. These places are not only marked by Spanish names, but also by "Spanish faces." The towns or name-places are not necessarily names of girls, saints, or towns in Spain, but are the names of particular places based on the geographical or natural setting, i.e. "Resaca" meaning surf or undertow; "Creston" meaning rock outcropping; "Celo" meaning rut; and "Valle Crucis" meaning valley of the cross-roads. Each of these present-day name places in northern Georgia and western North Carolina — Resaca, Georgia; Creston, North Carolina; Celo, North Carolina; and Valle Crucis, North Carolina are all descriptive of their setting as are many others. These places are not in the immediate vicinity of the original Pardo forts and towns. but they all fall along the migration routes taken by the predecessors of the Melungeons.

The first to migrate from their original fort were the thirty or so men who had been left behind by Pardo at Chiaha, present-day Rome, Georgia. Although the Coosas (Creeks) were for the most part desirous of having the Spaniards among them, their neighbors toward the west and northwest were a constant threat to these few pioneers. Probably within a few months after Pardo left them at Chiaha, these men journeyed north up the Conasauga River past Resaca, Georgia thirty miles northeast of Rome to Cauchi where they joined with the twelve men which Pardo left at Cauchi. Having joined forces the forty-two soldier/settlers moved farther up Holly Creek away from the Indian town and established their own community in the vicinity of Cool Spring and Hasslers Mill where they farmed the land and built the stone fort atop present-day Fort Mountain which they used as a place of refuge in times of crisis. This group remained in this locale for at least one or two generations and as they grew in numbers decided to relocate to less populated lands. As they moved out, they took a westerly direction turning their backs on the high mountains toward the east. Some undoubtedly remained where they were and established their own communities away from the Indian towns. They dared not return to the seacoast and the Spanish settlements having sworn before God to stay and hold the land.

Those headed west crossed the Conasauga River and followed the Chicamauga toward the Tennessee River. It appears that this group of Melungeons made at least one stop prior to reaching the Tennessee. North of Chicamauga Creek about twenty miles from its mouth in the vicinity of Ringgold, Georgia lies Sand Mountain. Haywood identified this location as one of the forts which the "whites" were forced to abandon by the Cherokees.[1] As previously mentioned the "whites" were allowed to leave the country in peace. The stone walls on Sand Mountain in Catoosa County, Georgia were examined by Philip Smith in 1956. In his report Smith describes the wall as follows: "This wall, or rather walls are in extremely good shape for most of its length. I am uncertain whether to use the singular or plural forms because short outlying sections of wall have been located which possibly may be directly related to the main section. This main part of the wall is approximately six hundred twenty-seven feet in length and follows a fairly even horizontal course at about the one thousand two hundred contour. Its two ends terminate in the vicinity of several rather steep bluffs. For most of its length the wall stands quite vertically on the fairly steep (approximately 45 degrees) slope, although in a few places it has partially crumbled. The thickness throughout is consistently in the neighborhood of one foot, while the height varies from about one foot to two feet at the ends to three feet to four deep in the central sections. In two places only, at the north end and in the middle, some small areas of outcrop (are) incorporated into the construction. The wall is composed of small irregularly shaped stones derived from the locality and rather skillfully laid in well-preserved tiers. The Sand Mountain wall or walls indicate a mildly serpentine construction whose shape is due to the contours and general form of the mountain rather than to any purposeful representational idea. It does not fit in with our ideas of defensive construction in spite of its position between two steep bluffs, since at this present height (and there is no indication by way of surrounding debris that it was ever much higher) it would in itself offer little resistance to attackers. Nor does it appear to fulfil any function as boundary line, property marker, or earth retaining wall. There was a homestead on the crest of the mountain until the end of the last century, when the land was taken over by the Federal Government, but this wall does not seem to have formed part of it, either in the way of an animal enclosure or a property line. Queries among local inhabitants of the district provided no direct information concerning the wall, except that one elderly resident states that it had always been them in his recollection.[2]"

Smith in this case did not suggest that the stone fort might be ceremonial in function, but he was very emphatic about it not being defensive works. During July of 1992, the author visited the site on Sand Mountain. Sgt Ronnie Shadwick of the Tennessee Army National Guard escorted me to the site. I asked Sgt. Shadwick, who was on military duty at the Catoosa Training Center, that if he was ordered to select a site for a fortification where would he place the fort? Sgt. Shadwick indicated that he was very familiar with the Sand Mountain Facility and that he would build a fort between the bluffs on the east side of the mountain, the very place where the stone wall stood. The author took special note of a large oblong cavity whose inner surface appeared to have been plastered to a smooth waterproof finish was in fact a "tinaja" or large earthen jar. When the author saw it, it held water one foot deep. Tinajas are very common in the arid southwestern region of the United States. They are natural cavities in canyons and arroyos and catch rainwater and hold it for long periods of time. The Apaches were able to survive and consistently outwit United States Cavalry troops because they knew how to live off the desert and always knew where to go for water, whereas the U.S. Cavalry's water supply was limited to the amount of water that they could carry. A network of tinajas was available to the Apaches and only they knew how to locate them. The tinaja at Sand Mountain is probably supplied not only by rain water but also by an intermittent spring located up the slope from the tinaja. The author did not view the spring, but a map of that area shows a "Rock Spring" near the top of the crest on the south side.

Below Sand Mountain about six thousand feet toward the southeast lies the verdant valley of Tiger Creek, not too far distant from Chicamauga Creek, where the Melungeons built their homes and tilled the fields using the stone fort on a temporary basis for defensive purposes. This group of Melungeons probably remained at this location until the Cherokees defeated them at the mouth of the South Chicamauga during the late 1600's where they were joined by other groups of Melungeons which had been driven down the Hiwassee and Little Tennessee Rivers from their other forts and settlements.[3] Also according to Haywood this larger group of "whites" moved westward into the hunting grounds of the Cherokee, Shawnee and Creeks. They coasted on rafts down the Tennessee River as far as the junction of Battle Creek and the Tennessee River where some of them disembarked and followed the broad canyon of Battle Creek which cuts deep into the heavily wooded Cumberland Plateau to its beginnings finally emerging near present-day Monteagle, Tennessee (Spanish for many or deep woods).

The route over which these seventeenth century Melungeons traversed was the ancient animal and Indian trail that linked the Tennessee River Valley of east central Tennessee with the present-day Nashville Basin. It was along this same trail that the late eighteenth century (1794) Nickajack Expedition traveled to make war on the Chicamauga Cherokee towns near Chattanooga, Tennessee.

From Monteagle, the Melungeons descended onto no-man's land. This region was the hunting grounds shared by many tribes since it was considered unsuitable for permanent habitation by

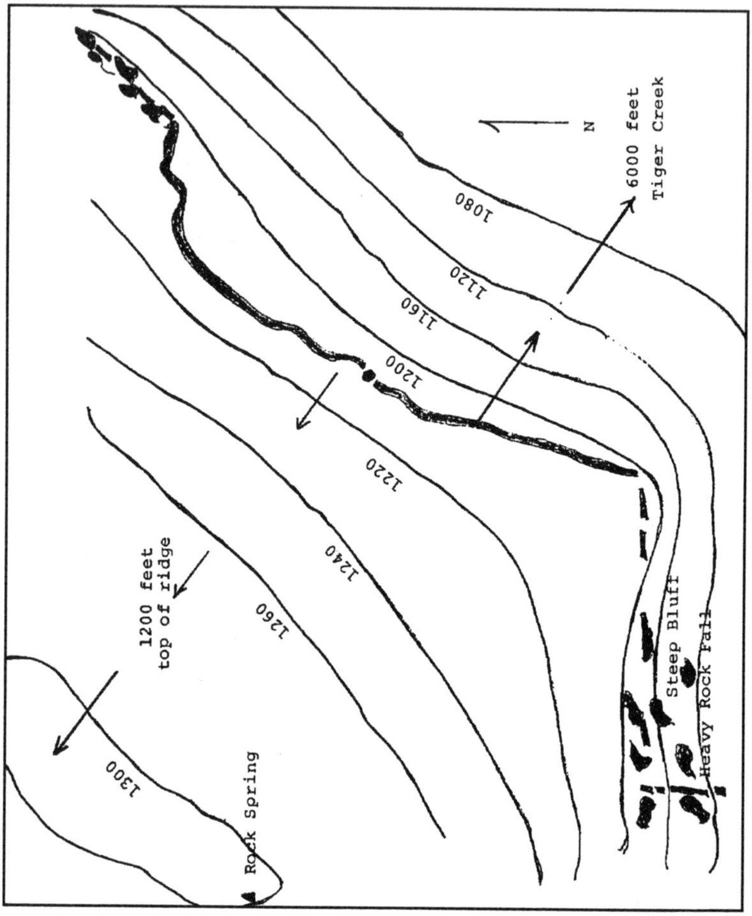

Figure 24. **SEVENTEENTH CENTURY SPANISH FORT SAND MOUNTAIN, CATOOSA COUNTY, GEORGIA**

Indians. At a later day it was called "The Barrens" in the vicinity of the Duck Rivers. The wandering descendants of Pardo's soldier/settlers having had enough of Indian wars and Indians found the area very suitable for a lengthy stopover. The geographical setting atop a high mesa guarded by high bluffs on three sides where the Little Duck River and the Duck River join was where the descendants of the Cauchi Melungeons constructed a stone fort five times longer than the fort atop Fort Mountain, Georgia. This group of Melungeons remained at the Old Stone Fort near present-day Manchester, Tennessee until the middle 1700's before moving into the Nashville Basin or westward along the Tennessee-Alabama line or back up on the Cumberland Plateau where they gradually crept northward through present-day Bledsoe, Rhea, Cumberland, Morgan, Anderson, Union, Grainger, Claiborne Counties on the west side of the Tennessee Valley and Bradley, Polk, McMinn, Monroe, Blount, Sevier and Cocke Counties on the east side of the Tennessee River.

The sprinkling of Melungeons from east to west and north to south in Tennessee left us with present-day name places and towns such as Angelico Pass, Isabella, Seravilla, Monteagle, Alto, Monterey, Del Rio, Santa Fe, Las Casas, Saltillo, Savannah, Yuma, Medina, Alamo, Pinson, Rhea, Atoka, Cordova, Bolivar, Bogota and Rives, not to mention those along the northern part of Alabama and Mississippi such as Francisco, Vina, Jacinto, Buena Vista, Saltillo, Byhelia, Hernando. Along with the Spanish name-places went the "Spanish faces" and surnames long corrupted into English. Two locations west of the Old Stone Fort at Manchester deserve special mention. One is in Giles County, Tennessee south of Pulaski, Tennessee. During one of the author's many visits to the Old Stone Fort State Park, I was informed by the then Park Superintendent that a stone fort somewhat similar to the one at Manchester had been discovered sometime back. The superintendent was reluctant to give the author any details regarding the find except that it was in that part of the State south of Pulaski. I asked him if he had knowledge of any Spanish artifacts being recovered in that area (Giles County)? He replied that some old Spanish coins had been uncovered some time back in the Fayetteville, Tennessee vicinity in neighboring Lincoln County. Both Lincoln and Giles Counties are traversed by the Elk River which has its origins in the vicinity of Old Stone Fort and at one point comes within ten miles of the Duck River. It is very possible that some of the Melungeons followed the Elk River on their western migrations. Those who migrated into the Nashville Basin probably found Frenchmen already in the area. Present-day Nashville, Tennessee has a large Melungeon population, although not many are ready to acclaim it as their heritage. A very popular Nashville Melungeon related surname, Goins, is also found in most counties east of Nashville in East Tennessee, Southwest Virginia, North Carolina, and Eastern Kentucky. The very name, Nash, as in Nashville, is a Melungeon related name. Some of the Nashes of Wise County, Virginia being of Melungeon origins were at one time referred to as "The Black Nashes."

The other site worthy of noting is the stone fortification at Cisco in Madison County, Tennessee in the vicinity of the South Fork of the Forked Deer River. Traces of ancient breastworks could still be seen above the ground in the middle 1800's as confirmed by "old settlers." Some of the Spanish name-places which have survived to the present-day are Cisco, Pinson, Bolivar, Saltillo, Montezuma, Cordova, Atoka, Medina, and Savannah. Southern Madison County could well have been along the Melungeon migration route westward. See Map on the following page.

The above discussion dealt with the descendants of the Spanish/Portuguese soldier/settlers which Pardo left behind at Chiaha and Cauchi on the western side of the present-day Blue Ridge Mountains of North Carolina and northern Georgia.

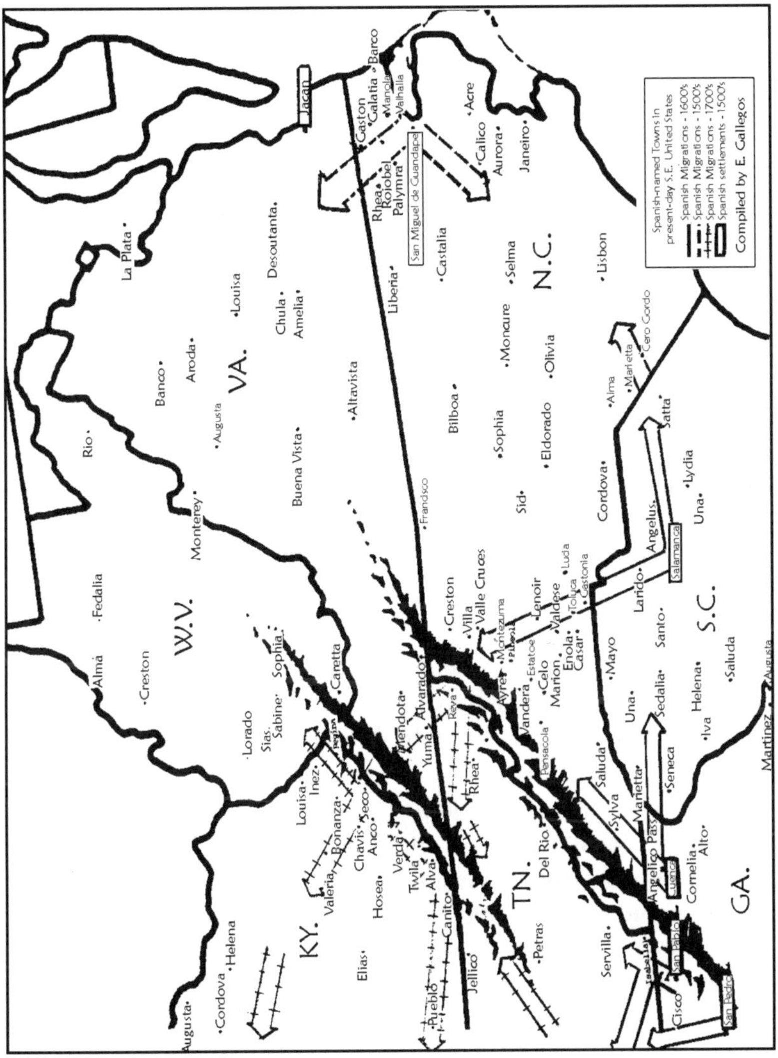

Figure 25. SPANISH-NAMED TOWNS IN PRESENT-DAY S.E. UNITED STATES

However, included in this group also were descendants of some of the men who were originally at San Juan de Juada and who joined the Chiaha (San Pedro) and Cauchi (San Pablo) Melungeons at a much later date having taken the long way around by way of the Hiwassee, Little Tennessee, and Tennessee Rivers before arriving at the Cherokee Chicamauga towns where they, too, were driven west with the Chiaha and Cauchi descendants by the Cherokees during the late 1600's. The group at San Juan de Juada probably remained intact in the Nacoochee Valley for one or two generations. Some of them were still in that area in 1597 when Pedro Fernandez Chozas, a Franciscan Friar, led a small party of Spaniards into present-day central Georgia. The purpose of the expedition was to reconnoitre the interior lands of Tama in order to find a suitable site for a permanent Spanish settlement. Chozas and party penetrated as far as the vicinity of present-day Atlanta, Georgia and reported sighting a "crystal mountain" (Stone Mountain). While in the vicinity of the crystal mountain, Chozas was informed by natives of the area that more than four days' journey toward the north beyond the "mountain" there lived men such as they who wore their hair short, used axes to fell trees and lived in houses.[4] The Nacoochee Valley where San Juan de Juada was situated about eighty miles from Atlanta or twenty miles/day.

When most of them departed they left at different times and in separate directions. Some probably remained in the Nacoochee Valley where as mentioned before continued mining along Dukes and Bean Creeks. Some of their descendants, the present-day Melungeons still reside in the general area. One group, the first to depart followed the Chattahoochee River northward past Spaniard's Knob over present-day Unicoi Gap to the headwaters of the Hiwassee River which they followed to its junction with the Valley River as it descends from the northeast through present-day Murphy, North Carolina. While in the Valley River Valley, they established mining operations much as they had operated in the

Nacoochee Valley. There are at least two accounts of non-Indians living in the area around Murphy, North Carolina prior to the arrival of English traders and settlers. James Mooney made note of two of these. Harry Smith, a half breed, born early in the 1800's and father of an East Cherokee chief informed Mooney that when he was a boy, he had been told by a very old woman that in times a "white" people had come to live for some time on the site of an ancient mound on the north side of the Hiwassee at the mouth of Peachtree Creek near Murphy. After a while they removed themselves and took the direction of the west. In the other account, an East Cherokee chief born at the beginning of the 1800's also informed Mooney that according to the history of his people, a race of white people lived near the Hiwassee opposite present-day Murphy. These people warned the Cherokee that they must not cross over to the south side of the river or a great leech in the water would swallow them. They, too, finally went west long before the coming of the English settlers.[5] That non-Indians were present in that area long before the English settlers arrived from the east can also be demonstrated by the remains of mining operations conducted by these "white people" (Melungeons). According to C.C. Jones in his *Antiquities of The Southern Indians*, evidence of very early mining in the Valley River Valley northeast of Murphy, North Carolina was reported by a Dr. Stephenson in his *Geology And Mineralogy of Georgia*, Atlanta, Georgia, 1871. According to Stephenson eleven old shafts had been found in the Valley River Valley vicinity. These ancient shafts varied in depth from ninety to one hundred feet. In 1854, one of the shafts was cleared of debris and at the depth of ninety-five feet a windlass of post-oak, well hewn, with an inch augur-hole bored (not burned) through each end was discovered. Distinct traces could be distinguished where it had been banded with iron straps. The crank and gudgeon-holes were very well preserved. A shaft that passed through twenty-five feet of gneiss-rock was scarred by the marks of sharp metal tools used in forcing the cut through the hard rock. No signs of blasting were in evidence, and below the water-level, the timbers and casing-boards and timbers were sound, although they had been discolored by the sulphurets of iron and copper.

Also discovered at that time were five other shafts similar in age and construction. These shafts were located closer to Murphy than the previous ones by about six miles. According to Dr. Stephenson, the trees growing in the mouths and upon the edges of these abandoned pits were not less than two hundred years old[6] which would have made the mines circa 1654 or earlier at about the time when some of the Melungeon families moved into that area from the Nacoochee Valley. When most of them headed west sometime around the middle of the 1600's, they journeyed down the Hiwassee River through the last cut in the upthrust of the Smokey Mountains of Tennessee into present-day Polk County where they fanned out westward along the Hiwassee River all the way to the Little Tennessee River where they were driven farther west and south to the mouth of South Chicamauga Creek where they and other Melungeons were defeated by the Cherokees but allowed to depart in peace, ultimately arriving at the junction of the Duck Rivers where they built Old Stone Fort near present-day Manchester, Tennessee. Those Melungeons moving north-south along the base of the Smokey Mountains left a people with "Spanish" faces and name-places such as Seravilla, Del Rio, Rhea, Isabella, Angelico, Alvarado and Rio Vista.

The other group of Melungeons to depart from the Nacoochee Valley rather than heading north up the present-day Unicoi Trail, followed the east-west trail which intersected the Unicoi Trail at the western end of the Nacoochee Valley. This trail ran from the Coosa River at Rome, Georgia to the Tugaloo River in the vicinity of Tallulah Falls where the Chattooga River flows in from the northeast mountains. Spanish artifacts of the sixteenth century have been recovered in the Tugaloo area of northeast Georgia. This group probably remained in the vicinity but a short time, after which some headed north through present-day Rabun Gap five miles north of Clayton, Georgia to the headwaters of the Little Tennessee River and thence down the Little Tennessee to the Tennessee River While others; followed the Chattooga River passing present-day Highlands, North Carolina on the east side and thence traveled along the eastern slopes of the Smokey and Blue Ridge Mountains moving in a northeasterly direction along the Indian trails. Spanish name-places abound along the eastern side of the Smokey and Blue Ridge Mountains in western North Carolina and northwestern South Carolina — Sylva, Saluda, Una, Senecca, Mayo, Celo, Pensacola, Vandera, Ayre, Estatoe, Montezuma, Casar. In addition to the name-places, a people called the Red Bones, and Brass Ankles, a regional term for the descendants of the Spanish/Portuguese settlers of the 1560's, reside in the northwest part of South Carolina although many of them migrated to Louisiana during the first three decades of the 1800's.

An old fort east of Asheville, North Carolina formerly called "Old Spanish Fort" can be attributed to the Spanish presence in the 1600's. As will be discussed later numerous Spanish artifacts of the sixteenth and seventeenth century have been recovered by archaeologists during the last four decades in Caldwell, Burke and McDowell Counties, North Carolina in the vicinity north of Old Spanish Fort. In the Fall of 1995 when the author was tracing the Spaniards' route up the Chattooga River in the vicinity of Highlands, North Carolina, a very interesting item was brought to the author's attention. High up on Whiteside Mountain on a narrow ledge on Devil's Courthouse is carved a mysterious inscription in Spanish which according to some long-time residents of Highlands has never been translated to make any sense. The inscription reads thus: "T.T. UN LUEGO SANTA A LA MEMORIA."[7] The author has translated this as "Testimony! An ordinary walk for the record." This was apparently carved by a person passing through the country wishing to leave a record of his having *Pase por aqui*. The above inscription was discovered by the first English settlers to move into Whiteside Cove more than one hundred fifty years ago.

Of the group that passed through Rabun Gap to the headwaters of the Little Tennessee River thence downstream to the valley of the Tennessee, they, too, can be accounted for as being present in that part of present-day Tennessee. By the middle of the 1600's, English traders were beginning to extend their territory beyond the Appomattox River at Fort Henry or present-day Petersburg, Virginia toward the southwest along the Occaneechee/Catawba trade trail. However, it was not until 1673 that the English from Jamestown, Virginia had any definitive knowledge as to what lay beyond the shining mountains toward the southwest into present-day Tennessee. One Abraham Wood, a member of Virginia Governor Sir William Berkely's "two hundred gentlemen" at a cost of one hundred forty-four pounds sterling sent out James Needham, Gabriel Arthur, eight Indians and four horses to penetrate the region of mystery that lay behind the mountain chains and on to the western water.[8] Two years prior in 1671, the same Abraham Wood had dispatched Thomas Batts and Robert Fallam to explore the wilderness west of Fort Henry, Virginia toward the Ohio River. Batts and Fallam followed the Roanoke River past the Blue Ridge Mountains to the Allegheny Mountains to the vicinity Matewan, West Virginia seventy miles short of the Ohio but they were convinced that they had seen "the ebbing and flowing water" of the western ocean (Pacific Ocean?).[9] The Melungeons would occupy these West Virginia lands within the next one-half century as we shall discuss later.

Needham and Arthur angled down from Fort Henry to Occaneechi Island in the vicinity of Clarkeville, Virginia where they continued south at a very slight angle from due west following a well worn Indian trail taking them along the upper reaches of the Yatkin River in upper North Carolina. Continuing more toward the west, they crossed the Blue Ridge at Deep Gap to Boone, North Carolina where two major Indian trails crossed in the vicinity of Valle Crucis (Valley of the Crossroads),very appropriately named. Their route took them north for a short distance past Villas (Villages) through a gap of the Alleghney Mountain between Zionville, North Carolina and Trade, Tennessee so low that one is not aware of passing over a major mountain ridge. After crossing the gap, Needham and Arthur turned south and crossed the Watauga River, the first of six major rivers flowing toward the northwest according to Needham's account. They then slid along the western base of the Alleghney Mountains crossing the Doe; Nolachucky, French Broad near Asheville, North Carolina; the Tuckaegee; and finally the Little Tennessee River which they reached at Lauada, North Carolina (Tombstone). Needham and Arthur followed the general course of the Southern Railroad of a later day. They always kept the smoke and haze of the Smokey Mountains on their right which they could see for a long distance before coming under their late afternoon shadow.

It was not long after that they reached the Little Tennessee River, which they followed westward, that they arrived at the major Cherokee Indian town of Tanasi upstream from Fort Loudoun State Park in Tennessee below where the river breaks through the upthrust. Tanasi is about one hundred fifty miles upstream from the Big Chicamauga Creek vicinity where the "whites" were then residing. Needham notes that during his visit to the Indian town which he called the Tomahittan town, it was brought to his attention by the leaders of the Tomahittans that eight days' journey (about one hundred sixty miles) down the river lived a white people who had long beards and whiskers and wore clothes, and that on some of the other rivers also lived those hairy people. Additionally these white people have a large bell which they ring morning and evening and at that time large numbers of people congregate together and talk in a strange language.[10] It is the custom in Spanish Catholic communities to ring the church bell in the morning to summon people to Mass or morning prayer and in the evening at 6:00 P.M. for the Angelus Hour. For many centuries these prayers were prayed in Latin. As a child, the author lived but a few blocks from St. Francis Cathedral in Santa Fe, New Mexico and can recall very vividly having to stop play of other activity and taking a few minutes every evening at 6:00 P.M. to say a few prayers in Latin. The author to this day can still recite those prayers by rote even though very few Latin prayers, if any, are still recited in Catholic worship.

Although the account is given by Needham, it was written by Abraham Wood in the form of a letter to a Sir John Richards in London, England. Wood states: "...not many yeares since ye Tomahitans sent twenty men laden with beavor to ye white people; they killed tenn of them and put ye other tenn in irons, two of which tenn escaped and one of them came with one of my men (Needham) to my platation. As you will understand after a small time of rest one of my men (Needham) returnee with his horse, ye Appomatock Indian and twelve Tomahitans, eight men and foure women. One of those eight is hee which hath been a prisoner with ye white people; my other man remaines with them untill ye next returne to learn ye language. The 10th of September my man with his horse and ye twelve Indians arrived at my house praise bee to God; ye Tomahitans have a bout sixty gunnes, not such locks as oures bee, the steeles are long and channelld where ye flints strike..."[11] Wood also adds that the Tomahittans had many brass "potts" and kettles from three to thirty gallons. After a short stay at Fort Henry, Needham set out again for the Shining Mountains but was killed by Indian John somewhere along the trading path, but not before bringing back information concerning the presence of the descendants of the Pardo people. The guns which the Tomahittans brought with them to Fort Henry, according to Wood, were not of English make. They could not have been of French origins since at about the same time that Needham and Arthur were entering Tennessee lands, the French under Marquette had just discovered the Mississippi River. The guns, pots, and kettles were possibly of Spanish make and origin. The men of Pardo's expedition were not only intrepid and loyal, but they were also skilled in the various trades including metallurgy. Needham's account of white people in the vicinity of Chattanooga, Tennessee corroborates with the tradition respecting the presence of a "white races" in that area of Tennessee handed down by the Cherokees to various Englishmen at different times. Haywood certainly took note of that in his *Natural and Aboriginal History of Tennessee*. Haywood also relates that these white people being finally defeated by the Cherokees at the mouth of Big Chicamauga Creek were allowed to depart for the west in peace as stated previously in this volume.[12]

The final group to be discussed are the soldier/settlers left behind by Pardo at Guatari in the vicinity south of Rock Hill, South Carolina. They, too, like their counterparts at Chiaha, Cauchi and Juada either headed north and west or melted into the back country away from the Indian communities and definitely away from the Spanish settlements on the Atlantic Seaboard. Those headed north and west eventually were joined by the San Juan de Juada people who headed up the Indian trail along the east side of the Smokey Mountains to the vicinity of Asheville, North Carolina using the same route which Needham and Arthur followed during their 1673 trek, except in reverse. The Spaniards at Guatari probably continued to have contact with the Atlantic Seaboard settlement of Santa Elena on Port Royal Island since Guatari, or Salamanca as the Spanish called it, was more accessible than the other three Pardo settlements. Consequently their numbers were augmented by additional soldier/settlers during the period 1666 to 1686 while the Spanish were still at Port Royal Island. In addition to soldier/settlers, provisions and supplies also arrived at Salamanca on a more or less regular basis.

The Spaniards at Salamanca began trickling away from the original Pardo settlement at a very early date since it was not long after their arrival that news of mines toward the north reached them. Once the Spanish soldiers and settlers were removed from Santa Elena to San Agustin in the middle 1680's, communication between the Spanish in the interior and those along the Atlantic Seaboard ceased. In 1601, one Juan de Lara, a veteran soldier of the early Georgia-South Carolina Spanish frontier was ordered by Governor Canzo to investigate the presence of non-Indians toward the north. Lara made a wide swing from Guale (Georgia) to Orista (Carolinas) as far north as the vicinity south of Rock Hill, South Carolina but found no non-Indians. The Spaniards and their families having already left Guatari by 1601 were settled in at least three communities in present-day North Carolina along the Catawba River and some of its tributaries. In his manuscript on file at the Smithsonian Institute, Reinhardt gives detailed descriptions of evidence of early mining operations in northern South Carolina in the vicinity of King's Mountain well before the arrival of the English in that part of the State. Reinhardt writes: "Near King's Mountain there had been some discoveries made which go to show that mining had been attempted at an early date, and nearby is a small mountain called La Boon to this day, and this was the name of one of De Soto's generals."[13] Reinhardt uses as his sources Revolutionary War soldiers and aged relatives. His works are on file in the Bureau of American Ethnology in Washington, D.C. The author is not aware of De Soto having a general by the name of La Boon, however the author is certain that De Soto was not in the vicinity of King's Mountain as his route took him much farther toward the west. The Spaniards who were present in that part of the South Carolina-North Carolina country during the 1500's were Pardo's men, not De Soto's. These Iberians left many name-places bearing Spanish names which to this day appear on maps, i.e.

Calabash (Calabasa), Toluca, Casar, Valdese, Cordova, Lando, Santo, Angelus, Una, Mayo, Sedalia, Helena, Cid etc.

Another account of early mining in that part of the Southeastern United States is given by James Mooney as follows: "Very recently remains of an early white settlement, traditionally ascribed to the Spaniards, have been reported from Lincolnton, North Carolina, on the edge of the ancient country of the Sara among whom the Spaniards built a fort in 1566.

The mining works included a dam or cut stone, a series of low pillars of cut stone, arranged in squares as though intended for foundations of, a stone-walled well, a quarry from which the stone had been procured, a fire pit, and series of sinks, extending along the stream in which were found remains of timbers suggesting the subterranean cabins on Dukes Creek. All these antedated the first (English) settlement in that region, about the year 1750. Ancient mining indications are also reported from King's Mountain, about twenty miles distant..... The Spanish miners of whom Lederer heard in 1670 and Moore in 1690 were probably at work in this neighborhood."[14] The person, Lederer, to whom Mooney alludes was one Johannes Lederer, a German traveler who visited North Carolina and Virginia for purposes of writing about those lands. Lederer's account was written in Latin and he asserts that at the time he was present in that country, Spaniards were then working gold and silver mines in the Appalachian Mountains. He states that he saw actual specimens of the ore which the Indians showed him, and which they stated were being mined by Spaniards. Lederer brought samples of the ore back with him on his return to civilization. He adds: "Had I had with me half a score of resolute youths who would have stuck to me, I would have pushed on to the Spanish mines."[15] Undoubtedly Johannes Lederer had no desire to be taken by the Spaniards and impressed to working the mines. No less than six scholars have attempted to trace Lederer's route in North Carolina. In the author's opinion, Alan Vance Briceland in his *Westward From Virginia*, 1987, comes the closest to identifying the route. The author has studied the materials available and visited the sites, and in his opinion Lederer's Ushery where he turned back was not at the junction of the Deep and Haw Rivers but at the junction of the Rocky and Pee Dee Rivers in the vicinity of Town Creek, the site of an Indian village which was active when the Spaniards first made contact with the natives. Lederer decided to turn back at Ushery after the locals informed him that two and one-half days' journey from there to the southwest, a powerful "nation of bearded men" were seated, which Lederer supposed to be Spaniards.[16] Two and one-half days toward the southwest would have brought him to the vicinity of King's Mountain and the Spanish mines.

Lederer decided not to return along the same route by which he had approached Town Creek, or Ushery, wishing to avoid the troublesome marshy area on this return. Instead he set his course more easterly, and after traveling thirty to forty miles toward the northeast he fell into a "barren sandy desert." Thirty to forty miles east of and slightly north of Town Creek lies an extensive area of sand hills southwest of Southern Pines, North Carolina west of Fayetteville. Twenty years later in 1690 a Mr. James Moore on his way inland to establish trade with the natives in the Appalachian Mountains was informed by Indians in the Town Creek vicinity that Spaniards were working mines in the area at a distance of no more than twenty miles. These people went as far as to describe the bellows and furnaces used by the Spaniards and offered to conduct him to the location. Moores's guides thought little of the idea of intruding on the Spaniards so the visit to the mines was put aside. Subsequently, Moore attempted to lead a party to the Spanish mines, but the scheme failed to materialize.[17] These mines, too, were probably the King's Mountain or Lincolnton mines. Lincolnton, North Carolina is situated along the South Fork of the Catawba River. Spanish name-places such as Mariposa, Waco,

Lucia, Miranda, Gastonia, Plaza, Casar, Toluca, Ora, Sedalia, Marion and Honea abound in that part of the country around the King's Mountain Lincolnton vicinity.

But not all the Spanish/Portuguese settlers remained in that part of the country to engage in mining operations. There is definitive evidence that a large group of the Pardo people moved far up the Catawba River and its tributaries as far as present-day Morganton, North Carolina as early as the late 1500's and settled there for a while during the 1600's along Upper Creek, eight miles north of Morganton. During the 51st Annual Meeting of the Southeastern Archaeological Conference, November 10-12, 1994, in Lexington, Kentucky a paper entitled *New Evidence of 16th Century Spanish Artifacts in The Catawba River Valley, North Carolina* was presented. In the author's opinion, this paper by David G. Moore and Robin A. Beck is one of the most significant documents pertaining to the Spanish presence in the Southeastern United States to come to light in the author's twenty-five years of research pertaining to the Spanish Pioneers in United States History. Heretofore the presence of early Spanish artifacts on an archaeological site in the interior of the Southeastern United States have been interpreted using two basic models. The first model being that the Spanish artifacts were the result of direct or indirect trade between Spaniards and the resident population. The second being elite usage of high prestige Spanish materials and their subsequent interment, or stated another way, elite chiefs of the region obtained the material from related chiefs outside the immediate region. Moore and Beck introduced a third possibility; it being that the assemblage of artifacts recovered at the Burke County site consisting primarily of utilitarian ceramics, items did not fit the current models regarding trade goods.[18] Moore who is with the North Carolina Office of State Archaeology in Asheville supports a third option or model, it being that the domestic assemblage at the Berry site in Burke County, North Carolina suggests trade was not involved but, rather, resulted from a direct and longer term presence by Spaniards at the site although he was unable to frame the third option in a proper manner, i.e. lack of verifiable historical data that the Spanish were in that part of the interior Southeastern United States.[19] In fact several historical archaeologists at leading universities in Tennessee, Georgia, South Carolina and North Carolina steadfastly refuse to even consider that possibility. "Spaniards in the interior of our precious State! Never!" One University of Tennessee archaeologist was quoted as stating rather emphatically: "I will not believe that any Spaniards were ever in this part of the interior unless I uncover one wearing his armor, mounted on a horse."

The widely held, unfounded belief that all of the original Pardo settlements were overrun by Indians has precluded the acceptance of the reality that the first Melungeons sprung from the Pardo people. Henry Savage states in his book referring to the Pardo settlements: "Some men were killed, some drifted back down the trail when the Captain (Pardo) failed to return." Douglas Summers Brown adds: "Others including a fifer with his wife and children stayed and threw in their lot with their Indian hosts. Bayano himself returned to Santa Elena only to be tomahawked by an Edisto Indian." Some undoubtedly were slain. None drifted back to Santa Elena as they dared not. Summers uses as an example Sgt. Bayano as one who drifted back. Bayano made his exit at the same time that Pardo made his. Further, Pardo made no promise nor had any intention of returning to the interior. His orders to the soldier/settlers were to hold the land, a promise to which they swore under oath. They dared not return to the coast.

Ironically, the original Pardo sites and their assemblage of artifacts were not the key to significant Spanish presence in the interior of the Southeastern United States at that very early date. The key pieces to the puzzle lay in the far northwest corner of North Carolina in the upper Catawba and Yadkin regions. Neither De Soto nor Pardo ever ventured into that region as neither of them personally set foot in either present-day North Carolina or East Tennessee. Archaeologists in Georgia and South Carolina have unsuccessfully attempted to trace both De Soto's and Pardo's routes by using assemblages of artifacts found here or there. The beginning point for such historical research is a thorough "research of the literature" which includes memorials, ship's logs, maps and charts. Only after the historical researcher has studied the verifiable historical data should an attempt to trace a route be undertaken. Once having laid out the route, then and only then should the researcher begin to look for anthropological/archaeological evidence by extended visits to every mile of the route. The Spaniards were avid record keepers. There is no lack of written accounts or maps to the experienced researcher who is able to translate Spanish, Portuguese, Latin, French or Italian, the languages in which the history of the 1500's in the New World was recorded by contemporaries to the events. Only then can the historian place ceramics and other associated artifacts in their proper historical perspective.

Ceramics, associated classes of artifacts, and a few radio carbon dates have for a long time indicated that an extensive late prehistoric and proto-historic population existed in the Upper Catawba and Yadkin regions. Although artifact assemblages and other archaeological characteristics corresponded with Spanish accounts, no definitive data of a Spanish presence in the settlements had surfaced;[20] not until 1994 when archaeologists from North Carolina took another look at the site on Upper Creek, a tributary of the Catawba, eight miles north of Morganton, North Carolina. The first visit of the Berry site on Upper Creek was in 1986 at which time two areas of the four acre site were excavated and from which a large number of artifacts were recovered. During the 1994 surface collections of ceramics at the Berry site, fragments of Spanish olive jars were recovered.[21] In addition, a subsequent re-analysis of the ceramics excavated in 1986 were re-analyzed and several sherds which had previously been classified as "unidentified historic" were found to be Spanish olive jar. Spanish olive jars are the most common ceramics found in Spanish colonial sites in the New World. They span a time period from the 1490's through the 1700's. The primary use of these amphora-like vessels was for storage and transport of olive oil and wine. Once having been drained of their liquid contents the jars were used for dry storage and transport of olives, lard, condiments, beans and chick peas. Early style olive jars range from 1500-1570; middle-style range from 1560-1799 and were replaced by a late style jar by 1800. Although common throughout Florida and along the coastal areas of the Atlantic Seaboard including the Santa Elena vicinity, very rarely had they been found in the interior of the Southeast making the find on Upper Creek a very significant breakthrough. According to Moore what is even more significant is that none of the Berry site sherds had been altered to non-utilitarian form such as ear spools or gaming disks etc. Moore states that none of the Spanish ceramics yet recovered from the Berry site shows sign of such alteration may indicate the disposal of utilitarian waste, i.e. permanent or longtime residence.[22]

Two other types of Spanish sherds were also found on the surface and identified as Caparra Blue Majolica. This small carinated vessel otherwise known as albarelo, or drug jar, with a chronological (New World) range of 1492 to 1600, although never common, has been found mostly in Mexico, Central America, Venezuela and most recently at the Santa Elena vicinity and 16th century San Agustin. The third identifiable Spanish sherd found on the surface in 1994 was identified as Grayware by Stanley South and Chester DePratter of South Carolina.[23] The sherd recovered from the Berry site is very similar to examples recovered from the 16th century Franciscan mission settlement of Escamacu located at the extreme lower end of Parris Island, South Carolina where Stanley South has been "digging" since the 1970's being joined by

Chester DePratter in more recent times. The author joined South and DePratter in their Spring of 1996 "dig" at Parris Island. The author also visited the Berry site twice, the last time in the Fall of 1996 when the owner of the property acted as tour guide pointing out where the Indian mound almost ten feet high had been before being bulldozed in the 1960's. At that time uncontrolled recovery of numerous sherds laying on the surface of the ground in the immediate area of the mound site occurred. The entire collection of historic artifacts from the Berry site totaled twenty-six. Included are twelve potsherds, one iron knife, three nails, one cut spike, three gun flints, one glass bead, one piece of melted lead, two buttons, one rolled brass bead, one piece of strap iron, and a piece of unidentified metal (perhaps pewter). According to Moore, ten of the twenty-six are 1700's or later, the remaining sixteen are at least 16th century Spanish artifacts from the late 1500's and early 1600's. The late 16th century and early 17th century artifacts other than sherds include one large wrought nail, a piece of melted lead, one glass bead, and one rolled brass bead. Stanley South of the University of South Carolina identified the nail recovered during the 1994 surface investigations as distinctive of 16th century forms, and added that Spanish nails are characterized by a flat to domed head, with some, of the rose heads appearing like toad stools. The melted shot which was recovered during the 1986 excavations, heavily patinated; appears to have been altered in the same manner as an example recovered from the Franciscan Mission settlement on Parris Island, South Carolina. The opaque blue bead found on the surface was similar to others which have been recovered throughout the Southeastern United States from contexts dating to the latter half of the 1650's. The final artifact, the rolled brass bead recovered during the 1960's when the Indian mound was bulldozed, is similar to beads of that type which were of the earliest form of brass ornament recovered from the interior Southeast, and although they are usually associated with the 1600's, they are occasionally found on sites with early 1550's components. Of the other artifacts which are not clearly 16th century, according to Moore it is unlikely that these items except possibly for the iron knife, predate European (English) settlement of the area in the 1760's. By this time most of the Melungeons had departed and were already situated in upper East Tennessee, Southwest Virginia, and Eastern Kentucky.

Although Moore was unable to ascertain a reliable date for the knife due to lack of better comparative data, he leaned toward a date in the 1600's and possibly 1500's. The knife itself was recovered from definite undisturbed context excavated in 1986. The knife was placed on the chest of an adult male. Along with the knife other burial items included triangular arrow points, a turtle carapace, a large corner notched blade, a stone-working toolkit, and a ceramic elbow pipe with soapstone tempering and copper disks, possibly ear spools, were located over each parietal. Although the knife displays similar characteristics to a late 1500's and early 1600's knife recovered in the northeastern part of the United States, not enough data was available to establish a definitive date. Moore states: "We are unable to ascertain a reliable date without better comparative material. However, the burial context seems to support a pre-18th century, i.e. 1600's or earlier."[24] Most of the Spanish artifacts assemblages are from Burke County, however, two other surrounding counties, McDowell and Caldwell Counties have also produced artifacts which possibly date to the 1500's and 1600's.

The descendants of Pardo's soldier/settlers, the Melungeons, probably remained in that area of North Carolina for three generations and as their numbers increased, they began to disburse in all directions except east, the direction from which the English were arriving. Although most went north toward upper East Tennessee and Southwest Virginia, some melted into the surrounding country isolating themselves from the Indians and English settlers. In the meantime that branch of the San Juan de Juada Melungeons who followed the eastern side of the Smokey and Blue Ridge Mountains were also creeping farther north past present-day Asheville, North Carolina. They, too, were leaving small groups or individual families isolated in the countless ridges and hollows of the Smokey and Blue Ridge Mountains where they still reside to the present day. The author has visited many of those remote places with names such as Saluda, Sylva (Silva), Celo, Marion, Valdese, Toluca, Lenoir, Pineola, Montezuma, Ayre, Vandera, Valle Crucis, Villas, Creston, Francisco, Neva, Rhea, Jalapa, Del Rio, Alvarado, Yuma, Mendota, Angelico and has looked into the "Spanish faces" of people who have wondered who they are. The heritage of these people embodies the struggle for existence of men, women, and children who have clung for centuries to a precarious foothold in a climate of hate and intolerance. Their heritage left us a people who have spanned the gap of time in a humble yet relentless day-by-day mode of survival in that lonely place between the light and the dark races.

VI

THE MELUNGEONS

By the later part of the 1700's, the descendants of Pardo's "The Few" were no longer Spanish or Portuguese. They numbered in the tens of thousands and had spread out over all of the Southeastern United States and Kentucky, Arkansas, Missouri, West Virginia, Ohio, Indiana and the Dakotas. They had become a melange, a mixture, which by the beginning of the 1800's included Scots, Irish, German, Dutch and possibly Turk. By 1715, they were already living and thriving as far west as Pound, Virginia in Wise County. No doubt many of them had begun to move west of Pound Gap into Letcher County, Kentucky where many of them still reside to this day. After crossing into Kentucky they spread out right and left along the isolated ridges and hollows reaching south toward Cumberland Gap (almost two generations before Daniel Boone led his settlers into Kentucky) and north into West Virginia and Ohio. In 1994, the author visited the Hancock County, Tennessee–Lee County, Virginia area which is home to large numbers of Melungeons. In fact, it was primarily from Hancock County and Lee County that the participants in the gene frequency analysis discussed earlier resided. One of the many off-the-beaten-path places that the author visited was the Blackwater Community of Lee County, Virginia. Less than six miles northwest of Blackwater over a low place on Powell Mountain and across

Wallen Ridge lies the route which pioneers coming west from North Carolina used on their approach to Cumberland Gap. The present-day road over the mountain follows the general route of an ancient game and Indian trail leading from the Tennessee Valley into Southwestern Virginia. A long-time resident of Blackwater took the author to a spot a short distance southeast of Blackwater where the road entered a cut between two ridges. About fifty feet off the road on the north side of Blackwater Creek stood an ancient tree which had been dead for so many years that only about thirty feet of its massive trunk still remained standing. About fifteen feet up on the southeast side of the trunk barely discernible was carved the year "1731" and an arrow directly above it pointing in the direction of the low place on Powell Mountain. The local resident also informed the author that at a distance down the creek was another ancient tree trunk with the same message. Four miles toward the southeast along the North Fork of the Clinch River lies the historic village of Doña.

Dr. Thomas Walker during this travels through Southwestern Virginia noticed cabins and a fort in the vicinity northwest of present-day Kingsport, Tennessee near Fort Robinson at the junction of the Holston and the North Fork of the Holston.[1] Not surprisingly, Kingsport, Tennessee has a sizeable Melungeon population. Spanish name places include Frisco, Yuma, Alvarado, Doña, Rio Vista, Rhea and Mendota. The Melungeons were already residing in upper East Tennessee when John Sevier (Juan Javier), destined to be the first governor, first came to the Watauga Old Field near present-day Elizabethton, Tennessee in 1771. He remained but a short time...and returned to New Market, Virginia where Valentino Xavier, or Javier, John Sevier's father had settled sometime during the first half of the 1700's. Valentino Javier's father had fled to England from France at the close of the 17th century due to religious persecution, first in Spain then in France. The Javier family came from the Kingdom of Navarre in the north of Spain.[2] Valentino's father probably came from Spain as a Spanish Huguenot.

John Sevier did not remain long at New Market as the very next year (1772) he was back in Tennessee seeking to go into business with Col. John Carter. Col. Carter's place was located on the Doe River near its junction with the Watauga near the present site of Elizabethton, Tennessee. During his second visit, he took note and commented on some of the residents. A review of the Draper Papers, presently in the possession of the University of Wisconsin in Madison, reported the following based on Sevier's observations: "Here was a race (of people) and Sevier seeing a large savage fellow of the name of 'Shote' (Chato, meaning pug nosed) take from a traveling stranger his horse, pretending he had won him in a bet when in reality the stranger never thought of betting.

(This) so disgusted Sevier that he resolved he could not think of settling among so villainous a people. On his return home, he met with Evan Shelby and told Shelby of this affair. 'Ooh' said Shelby, 'never mind those rascals. They'll soon take the poplar and push off.'[3] About 1780 this Shote was shot by some men in pursuit of him a noted horse thief." Sevier returned to East Tennessee, and at a later date he led some of those rascals into battle at King's Mountain during the American Revolutionary War. On the military roster listing the various backgrounds of enlistees such as Scot, English, etc. was also a category labeled "other." Melungeons not only fought under John Sevier during the War of The Revolution, but they also fought under the original South Carolina Gamecock, General Thomas Sumter, under whom they enlisted at that remote crossroads in back-country South Carolina. History has recorded the names of two such individuals. One Joseph Benehaly and another by the name of Scott who after the War were each given a piece of land by the Old General near his plantation at Stateburg, South Carolina. Anne King Gregorie, who in 1931 wrote a biography of General Thomas Sumter states: "Among his tenants were several named Scott, who are mentioned in his business letters; and there was one Benenhaly, a mysterious Ben Ali possibly whom tradition points to as the General's bugler during the Revolution, and whose family later intermarried with the Oxendines. Their descendants (Scott's and Benenhaly's) are now a group of some three hundred dark-skinned people, locally known as 'Turks' and 'Red Bones' in their community near Stateburg. They hold themselves aloof both from negroes and whites, and with their own church, school and cemetery, are as much a mystery to their neighbors as the mound builders."[4] Many of those Red Bones migrated to Louisiana during the first three decades of the 1800's where today many of them continue to live in isolation from the general population.

After the War of The Revolution, once the western lands were declared open, the movement west began and lasted for almost a century. As a general rule, the Melungeon movement west coincided with the western migration of the Revolutionary War soldier going west to claim his Bounty Lands. Once the Melungeons exploded into Eastern Kentucky through the gaps in the front rim, they moved into the remote areas north and south leaving Spanish name-places as a reminder of their presence. Names such as Pueblo, Capito, Alva, Alma, Verde, Anco, Seco, Chavis, Bonanza, Valeria, Regina, Caretta, Sabine, Sias, Lorado. Not only did they leave name-places, but they left other cultural reminders. They left a type of music still played today with sounds of both Middle East and Western European notes. The dulcimer, the much acclaimed musical instrument of Appalachia, came to the Cumberland Plateau from Egypt where it had its origins by way of Spain and brought to the present-day Southeastern United States by the ancestors of the Melungeons who by 1800 had already resided in the Southeastern United States almost eight generations.

A cultural custom with which the author is very familiar is a peculiar way of burying some of the dead. The author has visited numerous Spanish Colonial towns of the 1500's and 1600's in Mexico, Central America, South America, Spain and the southwestern United States, primarily Northern New Mexico, where the practice of erecting open *portales* (porches) over the graves of the very rich and influential and the very, very young was common during colonial times. These edifices are called either Lapidas or Bovedas depending on the region in which they are located. The idea behind the Lapidas/Bovedas (some are very elaborate and ornate) for the very rich and influential is so that succeeding generations will know that the remains of the person lying under the edifice was "not just anybody." He was a Hidalgo. On the other hand the purpose of erecting Lapidas/Bovedas over the graves of the very, very young is so that their young tender remains might be protected from the elements. A custom which the author finds very touching regarding the very young is that on special occasions such as their birthday, Christmas etc., toys are placed over their graves under the Lapidas as a special act of love by those that the deceased left behind. During one of the author's many visits into the remote hollows and ridges of East Tennessee, Southwestern Virginia, and Eastern Kentucky, the author saw many such edifices. One that remains most vivid was the grave of a baby boy who lived less than two years. Under the Lapida were several toys, some old, some fairly new, but the one that caught the author's emotions was a very rusty two-wheeled scooter similar to the one that the author's parents gave him more than fifty-seven years ago on his 6th birthday in a remote Northern New Mexico village. The name on that grave marker was Sebastian. It was located on a steep hillside cemetery in Letcher County, Kentucky on the west side of Pound Gap, Virginia in Wise County.

The descendants of Pardo's Spanish settlers and their families who were forced to leave the Cherokee lands in the late 1600's in flatboats ultimately arrived in the Missouri River country in the vicinity of present-day Bismark, North Dakota. This group of

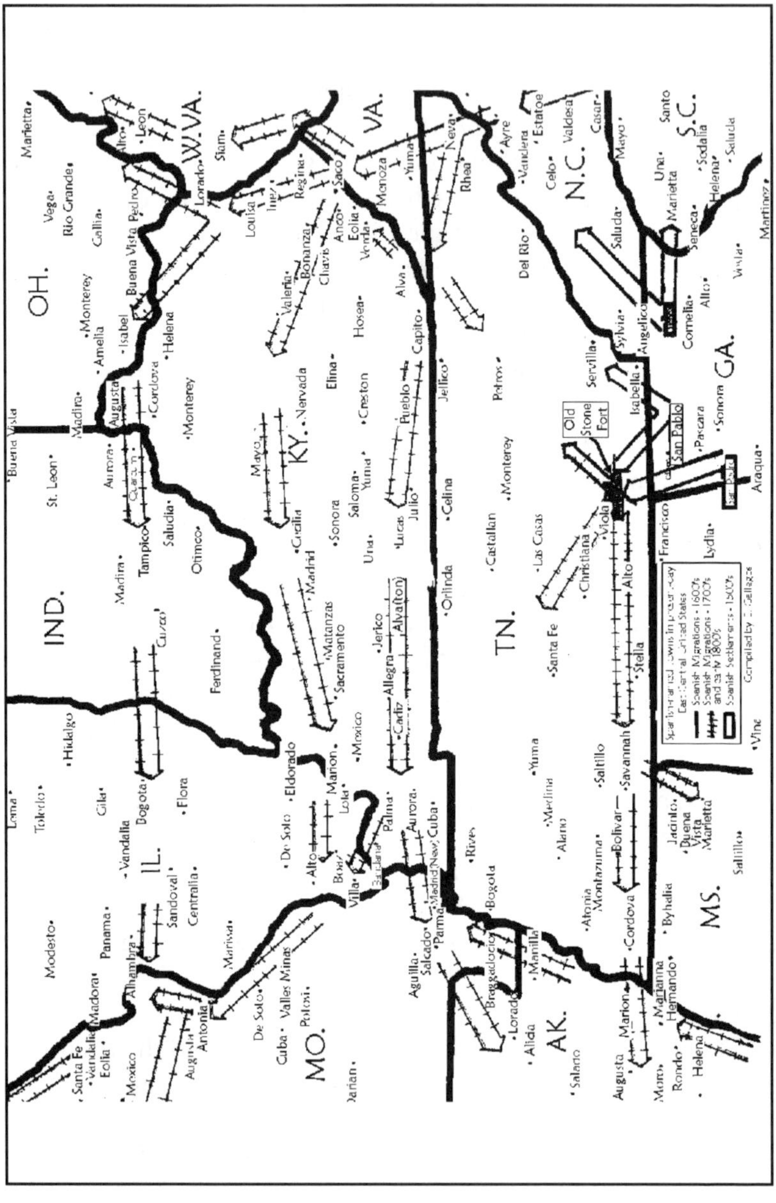

Figure 26. SPANISH-NAMED TOWNS IN PRESENT-DAY EAST CENTRAL UNITED STATES

Melungeons came to the Missouri River country by way of the Red River of the North and thence westward across the lands of the Sioux. Light-haired, green-eyed Crazy Horse of the Hidatsa Indians was probably descended from this group of Melungeons. This group will be discussed in another volume which deals with the Spanish pioneers in the Missouri country.

The Summer of 1997 in Wise, Virginia after more than four hundred years (fourteen generations) of living in isolation and oftentimes in denial of their heritage, the descendants of those few Spanish/Portuguese pioneers in the Pardo settlements assembled to share in their proud heritage, no longer to be the "Forgotten People."

The Melungeon-related names of the forgotten people who come from Tennessee, Kentucky, North Carolina and Virginia are: Adams, Adkins, Barker, Barnes, Beckler, Bell, Benehaly, Bennett, Berry, Biggs, Bolen, Bowlin, Bowling, Bowman, Branham, Brogan, Bullion, Burton, Byrd, Campbell, Carrico, Carter, Casteel, Caudill, Chavis, Clark, Coal, Coffy, Cole, Coleman, Coles, Colley, Collins, Collier, Collinsworth, Colyer, Counts, Cox, Coxe, Crow, Cumba, Cumbo, Cumbow Curry, Davis, Denham, Dorton, Dye, Ely, Evans, Faulkner, Fields, Freeman, French, Gann, Garland, Gibson, Gipson, Goins, Goings, Gorvens, Gowan, Gowen, Graham, Gwinn, Hall, Hammond, Hendricks, Hendrix, Hill, Hillman, Hopkins, Jackson, Keith, Kennedy, Kiser, Lawson, Lopes, Lucas, Maggard, Malloney, Martin, Minor, Miner, Mizer, Moore, Morley, Mullins, Nash, Niccans, Noel, Orr, Osborn, Osborne, Perry, Phelps, Phipps, Polly, Powers, Pruitt, Ramey, Rasnick, Reaves, Reeves, Roberson, Robertson, Robinson, Sexton, Shephard, Short, Sizemore, Stallard, Stanley, Steel, Swindall, Tharpe, Tolliver, Turner, Vanover, Watts, White, Whited, Williams, Willis, Wright, Wyatt.

The Brass Ankles-related surnames from South Carolina and North Carolina are: Boone, Braveboy, Bunch, Chavis, Criel,

Driggers, Goins, Going, Harmon, Jackson, Russell, Sammons, Scott, Shavis, Sweat, Swelt, William.

Red Bones-related surnames in North Carolina, South Carolina, and Louisiana are: Ashworth, Bedgood, Butters, Buxton, Chavis, Clark, Cloud, Doyle, Dyess, Gibbs, Goins, Hyatt, James, Johnson, Maddox, Nelson, Perkins, Pinder, Smiling, Strother, Sweat, Thompson, Ware, Willis, Wisby.

Lumbee-related surnames in North Carolina and South Carolina are: Allen, Bennett, Berry, Bridger, Briger, Brooks, Brown, Butler, Chapman, Chavis, Cole, Coleman, Cooper, Cumba, Cumbo, Cumbow, Dare, Dial, Graham, Harris, Harvie, Harvey, Howe, Johnson, Jones, Lasie, Locklear, Lowry, Lucas, Martin, Oxendine, Paine, Patterson, Powell, Revels, Sampson, Scott, Smith, Stevens, Taylor, Vicars, Viccars, Vickers, Wheeler, White, Willis, Williamson, Wood and Wright.[5]

The author has attempted to give these people an accurate account of their history and heritage. The continuing story of these people can best be told by them themselves once they have discovered their own poet.

Appendix A

NAMES OF INDIVIDUALS IN THE SANTA ELENA COLONY DURING THE 156O's AND 1570's

Antonio de Padilla
Diego Casca de Salazar
Gomez de Santillan
Alonso Martinez Espadero
Diego de Cumiga
Lopes de Sarria
Gomes Henao
Lope de Vaillo
Tomas Vernaldo
Alvaro Flores
Francisco de Hecija
Valtesar de Oserno
Alonso Diaz
Domingo Hernandez
Blas Palomar
Gaspar Perete
Prudencio Arrieta
Juan Mes
Juan Garcia
Miguel Molina
Domingo Lopes
Pedro Garcia
Pedro Aguilera
Marcos Garcia
Juan Fernandes
Pedro Solis
Juan Gomez Fialo
Andres de Simancas
Juan Martin
Simon Bega
Juan Calvo de Zamora
Francisco Olmos
Gonzalo Vicente
Andres Vigero
Francisco Rodriguez
Alonso Diaz
Antonio Ruiz
Caspar Arias
Niculas de Vurgos
Alonso Guerra
Francisoo Rico
Juan Remon
Diego de Orbina
Migual Palomar
Juan Jil
Francisco Deibar
Anton de Pena Vaira
Bartolome de Medina
Juan Navarro
Domungo Quadrado
Pedro de Arziniega
Hernando Silva
Juan Sanches Moreno
Pedro Santana
Pedro de Rueda
Juan Baldes
Ganzalo Herrera
Rodrigo Madera
Francisco Ecija
Gaspar Nieto
Andres de Viveros
Pedro de Arciniega
Francisco de Ybar
Franciso Molgado
Florian Mosquera
Juan de Noriega
Juan Batista
Alonso Torres
Cristoval de Uzeda
Alonso de Baena
Alonso Garcia
Diego de Cardenex
Pedro del Arrazabal
Juan de Rivero

Appendix B

FORT SAN FELIPE

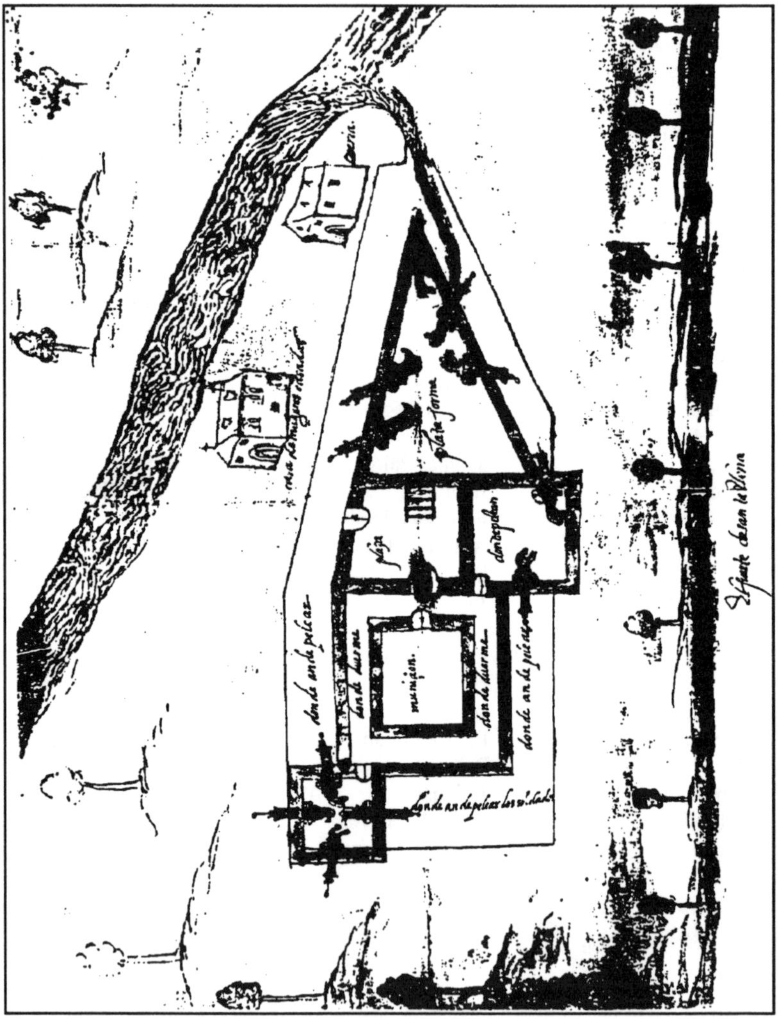

Figure 27. FORT SAN FELIPE—SANTA ELENA

Appendix C
Fort San Marcos

A sketch of the fort which accompanied the written report appears on the following page. The fort itself faced southerly toward the entrance of the harbor. As noted on the drawing several pieces of artillery were positioned in such a way so as to protect not only the harbor entrance to present-day Port Royal Sound, but also the approach up the Rio De Santa Elena (Beaufort River) on the east which was the approach commonly used by ships coming toward the fort and Santa Elena. That stretch of river between the south end of present-day Parris Island and Spanish Point was known as Canon de San Felipe. The drawing indicates that the place of disembarkation was situated on the south end of the fort on the "cano de ese rio" (inlet of that river). The cano being present-day Battery Creek which enters the Beaufort River from the west at the southeasternmost tip of Port Royal Island. Battery Creek wraps around the peninsula on the west on which the fort and town were built. Consequently, San Marcos was bounded on the west by Battery Creek. At that time during the 1570's, a pantano (marsh) lay between Battery Creek and the Spanish fort. On the south side of the fort where present-day Battery Creek enters the Beaufort River lay an estuary which made an excellent harbor for vessels. Across the small harbor toward the south was situated another marsh which today is the northern end of Parris Island, South Carolina, where at a later date the Franciscans built a church which was used as a visita (a satellite church and associated buildings of a larger mission) of the principal mission at St. Catherine's Island off of the Georgia coast. The visita on Parris Island (located on the present-day Marine Corps Center golf course) was active almost to the date of the entry into the Port Royal area by Englishmen from Barbados Island in the Lesser Antilles.

Toward the north of Fort San Marcos lay the city of Santa Elena between the forest and the fort itself. Around the entire fort lay a foso (moat), the water being taken from the "cano de ese rio" or present-day Battery Creek. The drawbridge over the foso was situated at the southeast corner of the fort. One entered the fort on the ground floor of a blockhouse where the soldiers stacked their arms. On the roof of the blockhouse were situated two cannon. One cannon guarded the entrance of "cano de ese rio" and the approach down the Rio de Santa Elena. The other cannon guarded the woods toward the east and northeast which stood between the fort and the Rio de Santa Elena toward the east. Three other cannon guarded over the city of Santa Elena and its vicinity. Although both the city and fort at Santa Elena would be deactivated within a few years, the footings and foundations of the town and fort would serve the Ingleses when they came to colonize the Port Royal vicinity during the late 1600's.

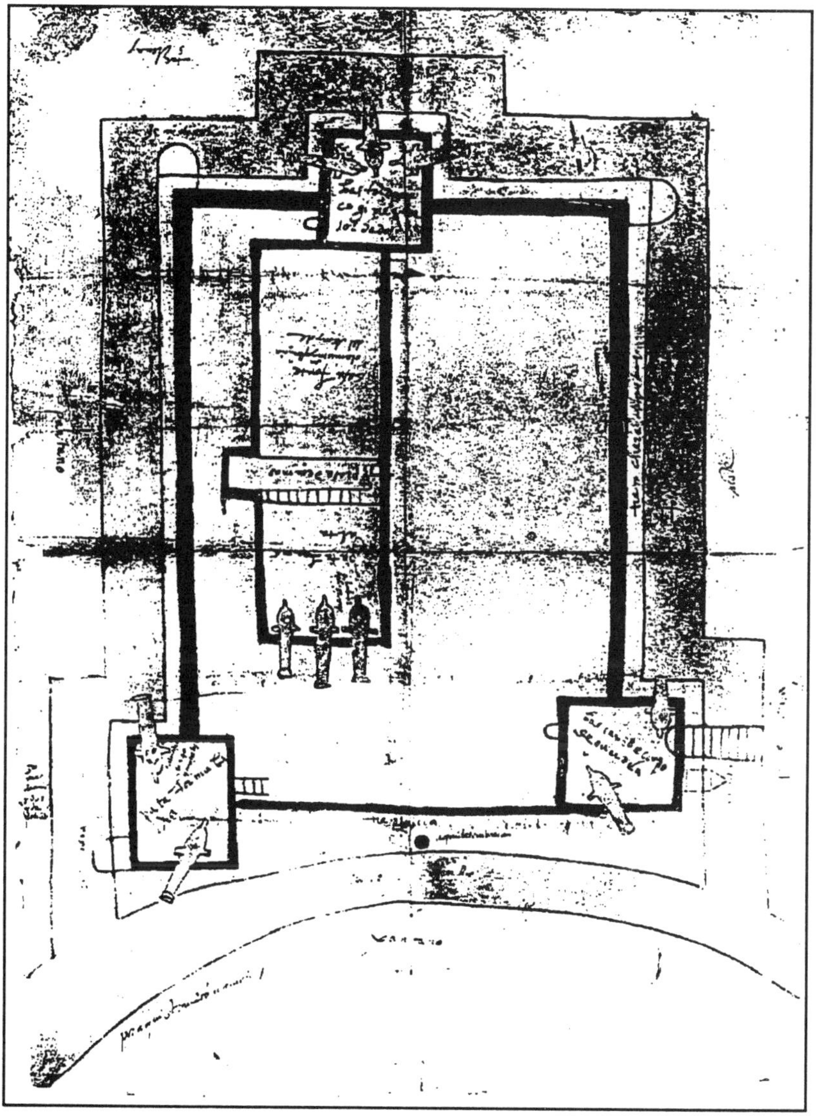

Figure 28. FORT SAN MARCOS—SANTA ELENA

Notes

THE HISTORY—LUCAS VASQUEZ DE AYLLON

1. Oviedo, Gonzalo Fernandez, *Historia General* etc., Vol. IV, pp. 325-326. Also, Navarrette, Martin, *COLECCION* etc. Vol. II, pp. 51-53.

2. Navarrette, Martin, *COLECCION* etc. Vol. II, pp. 51-53.

3. Ibid., Vol. II, p. 53.

4. Herrera, Antonio, *Historia General* etc., Vol. II, Capitulos, 8 and 9. Also, Navarrette, Martin, *COLECCION*, Vol. III., pp. 72, 73. and Vol. II, pp. 51-53. Also Oviedo, Gonzalo. *Historia General*, Vol. II, Capitulo IV, p. 333.

5. Alonso de Chaves, Alonso De Chaves Y El Libro De Su: Espejo De Navegantes, ed. Pablo Castaneda, M. Cuesta y p. Hernandez. Madrid, 1977, pp. 124, 125.

6. Orden del Gobernador D. Pedro de Ibarra (de San Agustin de La Florida) a el Capitan Francisco Fernandez de Ecija para reconocer las Costas del norte de Aquella Provincia Y Relacion de este viaje llevado por el mismo Capitan. Archivos General de Indias, Sevilla Est 2 Cajo 5; Legajo 8/16 Patronato.

7. See note 14 above.

8. Oviedo, Gonzalo, *Historia General*, Vol. IV, pp. 325, 326. Also Navarrette, Martin. *COLECCION*, Vol. II, pp. 51-53.

9. Ibid., Vol. IV, pp. 329, 330.

10. Ibib., Vol. IV, pp. 327, 328.

11. Ibid., Vol. IV, pp. 327-328.

12. Ibid., Vol. IV.

13. Navarrette, Martin, *COLECCION*, Vol. V, pp. 368-368.

14. Oviedo, Gonzalo, *Historia General*, Vol. V, pp. 368, 369.

15. Ibid., Vol. IV, pp. 327, 328.

16. Blacker, Irwin R. ed., *Hakluyt's Voyages*, Viking Press, New York, p. 290.

17. Ibid., p. 292.

18. Smith, John, 1608, A True Relation of such occurrences and accidents of noate as hath hapned in Virginia since the first planting of that Collony which is now resident in the South part thereof, til the last returne from thence., Narratives of Early Virginia. J.F. Jameson, ed., C. Scribner's Sons, New York, 1907, pp. 45, 49, 304.

19. Quinn, Beers David. *Set Fair For Roanoke*, University of North Carolina Press, Chapel Hill, 1985, p. 371.

20. Blacker, Irwin, *Hakluyt's Voyages*, pp. 294, 295.

21. Yeardely, Francis. *Narrative of Excursions Into Carolina, Narratives of Early Carolina*, F.F. Jameson, Ed. Charles Scribner's Sons, New York, 1911, p. 27.

22. Kennedy, N. Brent. *The Melungeons - The Resurrection of a Proud People*. Mercer Univ. Press, Macon, Ga., 1994, p. 111.

23. Ibid., *The Melungeons - The Resurrection*, etc., p. 120.

24. Quinn, David Beers. *The Roanoke Voyages*, Vol. I, Series 104. The Hakluyt Society 1952-1953, p. 251, 254, 255.

25. Terrae Incognitae 14, Wayne State Univ. Press, 1983, pp. 97-104.

26. Ibid., *Terrae Incognitae*, etc., p. 100.

27. Quinn, David Beers. *Set Fair For Roanoke*, Univ. of North Carolina Press, Chapel Hill, 1985.

28. Blacker, Irwin, *Hakluyt's Voyages*, Viking Press, New York, pp. 342, 372, 373.

29. Ibid., *Terrae Incogniatae*, etc., p. 99.

30. Ibid., *The Melungeons - The Resurrection*, etc., p. 112.

Notes

THE HISTORY—JUAN PARDO

1. Barcia, Andres Gonzales. *Ensayo Cronologico Para La Historia General De La Florida, Juan Ponce de Leon Hasta El Anno de 1722. Escrito por Don Gabriel de Cardenas Y Cano, Dedicado al Principe Nuestro Senor.* Con Privilegio: En Mardid 1723. p. 123.

2. Florida Ano 1609. Derrotero que hizo Andres Gonzales piloto en la Florida, del viaje que verifico por mandado de Pedro de Ibarra, Gobernador y Capitan General de aquellas provincia's de Xacan. AGI Sevilla, Simancas. Caj 8, Legajo 1/19 R 6/31 Patronato. Also Ecija, Francisco AGI. Sevilla, Simancas Caj 5: Legajo 8/16 Patronato. Also Conner, Jeannette Thurber, Colonial Records of Spanish Florida. Letters and Reports of Governors and Secular Persons. Deland. The Florida State Historical Society. MCMXXV, p. 51.

3. Ibid., p. 51.

4. Relacion de dos entradas hechas por Francisco (Juan) Pardo de La Punta Santa Elena, a Guatari Satapo llevando el camino de Zacateca, y de las vueltas, con memorial de una escursion hecho por un sargento bajo su mando. AGI. Patronato 19, R 22 (documento).

5. Memoria de Joan de la Vandera, en que se hace relacion de los lugares y tierra de la Florida donde el Capitan Juan Pardo entro a descubrir camino para Nueva Espana por los anos de 1566, 1567. Archivo de Simancas, Descripciones y publanciones 8. Copia sacada por D. Juan Baptista Munoz, Folio uno. And AGI. Patronato 19, R. 20.

6. Ibid., Memoria de Joan de la Vandera, Folio 1 verso.

7. Ibid., Folio 2 verso.

8. Relacion de dos entradas hechas por Francisco Pardo, AGI. Patronato 19, R. 22 (documento 1).

9. Memoria de Joan de la Vandera, Folio 2 verso.

10. Memoria de Francisco Martinez. AGI Patronato 19, R. 22 (documento 2) Folio 1 verso.

11. Autos sobre la relacion que dio el Capitan Juan Pardo de la entrada que hizo en tierras de la Florida. AGI, Santo Domingo 224. Folio 1 verso.

12. Ibid., Folio 1 verso.

13. Relacion de dos entradas Hechas por Francisco (Juan) Pardo etc., AGI. Patronato 19, R. 22 (documento 1).

14. El Capitan Juan Pardo - 1568. AGI, Contratacion 2929 No. 2, R. 7.

15. Autos sobre la relacion que dio El Capitan Juan Pardo etc., AGI. Santo Domingo 224 Folia 16 verso.

16. Ibid., Folio 9 verso.

17. Ibid., Folio 19 verso.

18. Ibid., Folio 25 verso.

19. Sevier and Madden, *Sevier Family History*. Special Collections University of Tennessee Library. CS715492.

Notes

THE HERITAGE—ORIGINS OF THE IBERIANS

1. Durant, Will. *The History of Civilization*. Simon and Schuster, New York, 1975. Vol IV, pp. 701-702.

2. Dromgoole, Will Allan. *The Melungeons*, The Arena 3, March 1891. Also *The Malungein Tree and Its Four Branches*, The Arena 3, June 1891.

3. Tennessee Anthropologist. Vol XV, No. 1, Spring 1990. p. 14.

4. Ibid., Tennessee Anthropologist, etc., p. 14.

5. Ibid., Tennessee Anthropologist, etc., pp. 20, 21.

6. Ibid., Tennessee Anthropologists, etc., p. 16.

7. Sumter, Thomas S., *Stateburg And Its People*, 1918. pp. 69-70.

8. U.S. Journal: Sumter County, South Carolina, New Yorker, March 8, 1964, pp. 104, 105.

9. North Carolina Reports, Vol. 169, Cases Argued And Determined in The Supreme Court of North Carolina, North Carolina Supreme Court Library, 1915, p. 25 (10).

10. The North Carolinian, Vol. 1, No. 4, December, 1955, pp. 107, 108, File no. T.O. - 105.1, State Department of Archives and History, Raleigh, North Carolina.

11. Ibid., North Carolina Reports, Vol. 169, etc., p. 11.

12. Yeardley, Francis. *Narrative of Excursions Into Carolina, Narratives of Early Carolina*, J.F. Jameson, Ed. Charles Scribner's Sons, New York, 1911, p. 27.

Notes

THE STONE FORTS

1. Smith, Philip E. *Aboriginal Stone Construction In The Southern Piedmont,* Report on field work in 1955 and 1956. Submitted to the Dept. Of Archaeology and Anthropology of the University of Georgia, October 1956, Peabody Museum, Harvard University, Cambridge, Ma., 1956. pp. 33, 34.

2. Ibid., *Aboriginal Stone Construction,* etc, p. 34.

3. Ibid., *Aboriginal Stone Construction,* etc., p. 42.

4. Faulkner, Charles. *The Old Stone Fort.* University of Tennessee, Knoxville, 1968. pp. 58-60.

5. Ibid., *The Old Stone Fort,* etc., pp. 23, 24.

6. Ibid., *The Old Stone Fort,* etc. p. 23.

7. Ibid., *The Old Stone Fort,* etc., p. 20.

8. Ibid., *The Old Stone Fort,* etc., p. 58.

9. Ibid., *The Old Stone Fort,* etc., p. 55.

10. Ibid., *The Old Stone Fort,* etc., p. 42.

11. Ibid., *The Old Stone Fort,* etc., p. 24.

12. Jones, Charles C. Jr. *Antiquities of The Southern Indians.* AMS Press, Inc., New York, 1973, p. 123. Also Mooney, James. *Historical Sketch of The Cherokee.* Aldine Publishing Co., Chicago, 1975. p. 36, 210.

13. Lumsden, Thomas N. MD. *The Nachoochee Valley.* Balok Printing Service, 1989, p. 4-5.

14. Ibid., *Aboriginal Stone Construction In Southern Piedmont*, etc., p. 15.

15. Ibid., *The Nacoochee Valley*, etc., p. 5.

16. Ibid., *The Antiquities of The Southern Indians*, etc., pp. 48, 49.

17. Ibid., *The Nacoochee Valley*, etc., p. 5.

18. Ibid., *Aboriginal Stone Construction In Southern Piedmont*, p. 23.

19. Ibid., *Aboriginal Stone Construction In Southern Piedmont*, p. 13.

20. Ibid., *Aboriginal Stone Construction In Southern Piedmont*, p. 13, 14.

21. Mooney, James. *Historical Sketch of The Cherokee.* Aldine Publishing Co., Chicago, 1975. p. 12.

22. Haywood, John. *Natural and Aboriginal History of Tennessee.* 1959 Edition, Jackson, Tennessee. p. 219.

23. Brown, Douglas Summers. *Catawba Indians - The People of The River.* University of South Carolina Press, Columbia, 1966. pp. 45, 46.

24. Ibid., *Catawba Indians*, etc., p. 45.

25. Ibid., *Historical Sketch of The Cherokee*, etc., p. 19.

Notes

THE PIONEERS

1. Haywood, John. *Natural and Aboriginal History of Tennessee.* 1959 Edition, Jackson, Tennessee, p. 219.

2. Smith, Philip E. *Aboriginal Stone Construction In The Southern Piedmont,* Report on field work in 1955 and 1956, submitted to the Dept. Of Archaeology and anthropology of the University of Georgia, October 1956, Peabody Museum, Harvard University, Cambridge, Ma., 1956, pp. 16, 17.

3. Ibid., *Natural and Aboriginal History,* etc., p. 219.

4. Carta de Canzo al Rey. 23 Fererro, 1598. AGI. Sec. V, ASD legajo 224. Also Carta del Rey a Canzo, 9 Noviembre, 1598, AGI. Sec. V, ASD leg. 222. Also Testimonio de varias personas a Don Gonzalo Mendez de Canzo, sobre la situacion de la Tama y sus requezas y de lapoblacion de inglesses. San Agustin, 4 de Febrero de 1600, AGI. Sec. V, ASD leg. 224.

5. Mooney, James. *Historical Sketch of the Cherokee.* Aldine Publishing Co, Chicago, 1975. p. 13.

6. Jones, Charles, C. Jr. *Antiquities of the Southern Indians.* AMS Press Inc., New York, 1973. pp. 48, 49.

7. McIntosh, Gert. *Highlands North Carolina - Early Explorers,* p. 21.

8. Wood, Abraham, *Letter of Abraham Wood - Giving Account of Nedham's Journey,* 1673. *Early Travels in Tennessee Country,* Watauga Press Johnson City, Tenn. 1938. pp. 24-38. Also Briceland, Alan Vance. *Westward From Virginia,* Univ. Press of Virginia, Charlottesville, 1987. p. 149.

9. Briceland, Alan Vance. *Westward from Virginia*, Univ. Press of Virginia, Charlottesville, 1987. p. 144.

10. Ibid., Letter of Abraham Wood, etc., p. 29.

11. Ibid., Letter of Abraham Wood, etc., pp. 29, 30.

12. Ibid., *Natural and Aboriginal History of Tennessee*, etc., p. 219.

13. Brown, Douglas Summers, *Catawba Indians -- The People of The River*, Univ. of South Carolina Press, Columbia, 1966, p. 45.

14. Ibid., *Historical Sketch of The Cherokee*, etc., p. 210.

15. Ibid., *Antiquities of the Southern Indians*, etc., p. 51.

16. Ibid., *Westward from Virginia*, etc., p. 122.

17. Ibid., *Antiquities of The Southern Indians*, etc., p. 51.

18. Moore, David G. *New Evidence of 16th Century Spanish Artifacts in the Catawba River Valley, North Carolina*, North Carolina Office of State Archaeology, Asheville, North Carolina, 1994, p. 3.

19. Ibid., *New Evidence of 16th Century*, etc., pp. 14, 15.

20. Ibid., *New Evidence of 16th Century*, etc., pp. 5, 6.

21. Ibid., *New Evidence of 16th Century*, etc., p. 6.

22. Ibid., *New Evidence of 16th Century*, etc., p. 10.

23. Ibid., *New Evidence of 16th Century*, etc., p. 9, 10.

24. Ibid., *New Evidence of 16th Century*, etc., p. 13.

Notes

THE MELUNGEONS

1. Walker, Thomas Dr., *Journal of An Exploration*, Little, Brown and Co., Boston, 1888. pp. 42, 43.

2. Sevier and Madden. *Sevier Family History*, Special Collections, University of Tennessee Library, Knoxville. Also *Draper Papers*, Univ of Wisconsin, Madison, Wisconsin, MSS 325140 and MSS 325210.

3. Ibid., *Sevier Family History*, etc.

4. Gregorie, Anne King PhD. *Thomas Sumter*, Press of The R.L. Bryan Company, Columbia, South Carolina, 1931. pp. 264-265.

5. Kennedy, N. Brent. *The Melungeons - The Resurrection of A Proud People*. Mercer Univ. Press, Macon, Ga. 1994. pp. 147-150.

BIBLIOGRAPHY

Main Sources and/or Documents

Arciniegas, C. Amerigo Y El Nuevo Mund. Editorial Hermes, Mexico, D.F., 1955.

Arredondo, Don Antonio de. Demostracion Historiographica del Derecho del Rey Catolico a Nueva Gorgia en Las Provincias y continente de La Florida en la que se prueva el dominio poscitivo que tiene el Rey de Espana haste la latitud septentrional de 32 grados 30 minutes inclusivos en que se halla la barra de la Isla Santa Elena, terming por el qual se deben arreglar los limites de las respectivas poseciones en esta parte de mundo entre La Florida y la Carolina. Havana en Marzo 20 de 1742.

Barcia, Andres Gonzales. Ensayo Cronologico para la *Historia General* de La Florida, Juan Ponce de Leon, haste el anno de 1722. Escrito por Don Gabriel de Cardenas Z Cano, Dedicado al Principe Nuestro Senor. Con Privilegio: En Madrid, 1723.

Barrientos, Bartolome, ca. 1518-1568. Pedro Menendez de Aviles. Reprinted by Univ. of Florida Press, Gainsville, 1965.

Basanier (editor) L' Historire Notable de la Florida situee en Indes Occidentales contenant les Trios Voyages Faicts en Icelle par certains Capitaines et Pilotes Francois Descrits par le Capitaine Laudoniere qui ia Commande L' Espace Dum an Trois Moys. Paris, 1586. Reprinted in Paul Gaffarel, Histoire de la Florida Francaise, Paris, 1875.

Cardenas, Juan de. Problemas Y Secretos Maravillosos de Las Indias. Impresa en Mejico, 1591. Reprinted in Ediciones Cultura Hispanica, Madrid, 1945.

Coleccion de Documentos Ineditos, Relativos De America Y Oceania sacados de los Archivos del Reino, y Muy especialmente del de Indias. Madrid, 1868.

Coleccion De Varios Documentos Para La Historia De La Florida Y Tierras Adyacentes. Madrid, Ano de l857.

Ecija, Fernandez Francisco de. Orden de Gobernador D. Pedro de Ibarra (de S. Agustin de la Florida) a el Capitan Francisco Fernandes de Ecija pare reconocer las costas del norte de aquella Provincia y Relacion de este viaje llevado a cavo por el mismo Capitan. A.G.I. Sevilla, Simancas Cajon 5; leg. 8/16. Patronato.

Expediente Sobre Los Asuntos De La Florida.
L G.I., Seville, Espana-Simancas. Autos entre Partes. Ano de 1560 a 1567. Estante 51; Cajon 6; Leg. 10/27, No. 2, R.L.

Garcia, Genaro (editor). Dos Antiquas Relciones de La Florida. Mejico, 1902.

Gomara, Francisco Lopez de (1510-1560). Historia De Las Indias. Tomo I. Reprinted Madrid, 1932.

Herrera, Antonio de. (1559-1625). *Historia General* De Los Hechos de Los Castellanos En Las Islas Y Tierrafirme Del Mar Oceano. Reprinted Madrid, 1936.

Hakluyt, Richard. Divers Voyages Touching The Discoverie of America, and the Lands adjacent. London, 1582. Reprinted by Ann Arbor Univ. Microfilms Inc., 1966.

Laudonniere, Rene. Three Voyages. Translated by Charles E. Bennet. The University Presses of Florida, Gainesville, 1975.

Laudonniere, Rene. A Notable Historie containing foure voyages made by certayne French Captaynes unto Florida. Translated by Richard Hakluyt. Thomas Dawson, London, 1587. Reprinted by Henry Stevens, Son and Stiles, New York, 1964.

Los Papeles De Luna, Documentos Referentes A La Expedicion De Don Tristan De Luna Y Arellano Para La Conquista De La Florida En 1559-1561. Deland, The Florida State Historical Society, MCMXXVII.

Martire, Pietro Anghiera de. The Decades of the Newe Worlde or West India. London, anno 1555. Reprinted by Ann Arbor Univ. Microfilms, Inc., 1966.

Martyris, Petri. DE NUPER, SUB D. Carolo Repertis Infulis, fimulge incolarum moribus, R. Petri Martyris, Enchiridion, Dominae Klargaritae, Diui Max. Caessiliae dicatum. Basileae, Anno M.D. XXI. Reprinted as Epitome De Pedro Martir by Juan Pablos (editor), Mejico, D.F., MCMLXXIII.

Margry, Pierre (editor). Decouvestes et Etablissements des Francais dans L' Quest et Dans le Sud de L' Amerique Septentrionale (1614-1754), Memoires et Documents Originaux recueillis et Publies Par Fierre Margry. Paris, MDCCCLXXXI.

Moyne, Jacques L'. Brevis Narratio. Frankfort, 1591. Translated by Fred B. Perkins and published as the Narrative of Le Moyne. Boston, 1875.

Navarrete, Martin Fernandez de. (1765-1844). Coliccion De Los Viajes Y Descubrimientos. Biblioteca De Autores Espanoles. Madrid, 1954.

Oviedo, Gonzalo Fernandez de. (1478-1552). *Historia General* Y Natural De Las Indias. Biblioteca de Autores Espanoles. Madrid, 1959.

Oviedo, Gonzalo Fernandes de, (1478-1557). De La Natural Historia De Las Indias. Editorial Suma, Madrid, 1942.

Ruidiaz Y Caravia, Eugenio. La Florida su Conquista Y Colonizacion por Pedro Flenendez de Aviles. 2 Vols. Madrid, 1893.

Ribaut, Jean. The Whole and True Discoverye of Terra Florida. London, 1563. Reprinted by the Florida State Historical Society, Deland, MCMXXVII.

Solis, Meras Gonzalo de. Memorial que hizo el Doctor Gonzalo Solis de Meras, de todas las jornades y succesos del Adelantado Pedro Menendez de, Aviles, su canodo, y de la conquista de La Florida y Justicia que hizo en Juan Ribao y otros Franceses. 1567. Reprinted In Ruidiaz o.p. cit.

Serrano Y Sanz, Manuel (editor). Documentos Historicos de La Florida Y La Luisiana. Siglos XVI al XVIII. Biblioteca de los Americanistas. Madrid, 1912.

Torquemada, Juar de. Primera (segunda, tercera) parte de los veinte in un libros rituales i monarchia indiana, con el origen y querras, de los Indios Ocidentales, de sus poblaciones descubrimiento, conquista, conversion y otras cosas maravillosas de la misma sierra Por F. Juan de Torquemada. Madrid, 1723. Edited by Andres Gonzales de Barcia y Zuniga.

Recopilacion de Leyes De Los Reynos De Las Indias. Ediciones Cultura Hispanica, 1973, Madrid.

MAIN SOURCES
Unpublished documents and/or Relaciones

Florida 1609, Gobernador D. Pedro de Ibarra (de S. Agustin de la Florida) a el Capitan Francisco Fernandez de Ecija para reconocer las Costas del norte de aquella Porvincia y Relacion de este viaje llevado a cavo por el mismo Capitan. A.G.I. Sevilla, Simancas, Cajon 5: legajo 8/16 Patronato.

Florida Ano 1609. Derrotero que hizo Andres nonzales piloto en la Florida, del viaje que verifico por mandado de Pedro de Ibarra, Cobe m ador y Capitan General de aquellas provincial de Xacan. A.G.I. Sevilla, Simancas. Florida Descubrimientos, descripciones y poblaciones de la Florida. Cajon 8, Legajo V 19 R 0/31 Patronato.

Ano de 1561. Relacion del Reconnocimento que hizo el Capitan General Angel de Villafane de la Costa de la Florida y posesion que tomo en el Rio de Santa Elena, Cavo San Roman, Los Rios de Jordan y de Cavo nombrado Trafalgar desde 33 haste 35 grados de altura N., Real Academia de la Historia, Madrid 16 RAH, 77-79.

Santa Elena 1569. Memoria de los lugares i sierra es cada luger de las provincial de la Florida por donde el Capitan Juan Pardo entro a decubrir camino para Nueva Espana desde la punta de Sancta Elena de las dichas provincial los ano de 566 (1566) i 567 (1567), que todo es como se sigue. R,eal Academia de la Historia, Madrid 15 RAH. 27-33.

1569. E1 Teniente gobernador de la Florida. Santo Domingo, primero de Abril de 1569. Autos para la Relacion que dio el capitan Juan Pardo de la entrada que hizo en tierra de la Florida. A.G.I., Santo Domingo 224.

Memorial de Francisco Martinez. A.G.I., Patronato 19, R.22 (documento 2), Folio 1 verso.

Other Books and/or Publications Consulted

Bolton, Eugene Herbert. *Coronado Knight of Pueblos and Plains*. University of New Mexico Press, 1949.

Bourne, Edward Gaylord, 1860-1908. *Spain in America, 1450-1580*. Harper and Brothers, 1904.

Bourne, Edward Gaylord, 1860-1908. *Narratives of The Career of Hernando de Soto in the Conquest of Florida*. Allerton Book Co., 1922.

Boyd, Mark Frederick, *Here They Once Stood*. Univ. of Florida Press, 1951.

Bridenbough, Carl. *Jamestown, 1544-1699*. Oxford University Press, 1980.

Brown, Alexander, 1843-1906. *The Genesis of The United States*. Houghton, Mifflin and Company, 1890.

Casas, Bartolome de Las, 1474-1566. *The Devastation of the Indies*. Seabury Press, New York, 1974.

Chatelain, Verne Elmo, *The Defenses of Spanish Florida*. Carnegie Institution of Washington Pub., Washington, D.C., 1941.

Caudill, Harry. *Night Comes To The Cumberlands*. Little Brown and Co., Boston, 1962.

Conner, Jeannette Thurber, *Colonial Records of Spanish Florida. Letters and Reports of Governors and Secular Persons*. Deland. The Florida State Historical Society, MCMXXV.

Corbitt, Leroy David. *Exploration, Descriptions, and Attempted Settlements, 1584-1590*. Raleigh, N.C., 1948.

Faulkner, Charles. *The Old Stone Fort*. Univ. of Tennessee, Knoxville, 1968.

Folmer, Henry, *France-Spanish Rivalry in North America, 1524-1763*. A.H. Clark Co., 1953.

Hanke, Lewis. *The First Social Experiments in America; a study in the development of Spanish Indian policy in the 16th century*. Harvard Univ. Press, 1935.

Hakluyt, Richard. *Hakluyt's Voyages*. The Viking Press, New York, 1965.

Haywood, John. *Natural And Aboriginal History of Tennessee*. 1959 Edition, Jackson, Tennessee.

Helps, Arthur, Sir, 1813-1875. *The Spanish Conquest in America*. John Lane, London, 1904.

Hodge. *Spanish Explorers In The Southern United States, 1528-1543: The Narrative of Alvar Nunez Cabeca de Vaca* Charles Scribner's Sons, 1907.

Hoffman, Paul. *A New Andalucia*. Louisiana State Univ. Press, Baton Rouge, 1990.

Jackson, William Richard, *Early Florida Through Spanish Eyes*. Univ. of Miami Press, 1954.

Jameson, J. Franklin, *Original Narratives of Early American History: Spanish Exploration of the Southwest, 1542-1706*. Charles Scribner's Sons, 1906-17.

Jameson, J. Franklin. *Original Narratives of Early American History: Narratives of Early Carolina*. Charles Scribner's Sons, 1906-17.

Jameson, J. Franklin. *Original Narratives of Early American History: Narratives of Early Virginia*. Charles Scribner's Sons, 1906-17.

Jones, Charles C. Jr. *Antiquities of The Southern Indians.* AMS Press Inc., New York, 1973.

Kennedy, N. Brent. *The Melungeons - The Resurrection of a Proud People*. Mercer Univ. Press, Macon Ga., 1994.

Lanning, John Tate, *The Spanish Missions of Georgia*. Univ. of North Carolina Press, 1935.

Lewis, Clifford Merle. *The Spanish Jesuit Mission in Virginia, 1570-1572*. Univ. of North Carolina Press, 1953.

Lumsden, Thomas N. MD. *The Nacoochee Valley*. Balok Printing Services, 1989.

Lowery, Woodbury, 1853-1906. *The Spanish Settlements Within The Present Limits of the United States*. G.P. Putnam's Sons, 1905.

Mooney, James.: *Historical Sketch of The Cherokee*. Aldine Publishing Co., Chicago, 1975.

Parkman, Francis, *1823-1893. Pioneers of France in The New World*. Little Brown and Co., 1907.

Parry, John Horace, *The Spanish Theory of Empire in the Sixteenth Century*. Folcroft Press, 1969.

Porter, Charles Wesley, *Fort Raleigh National Historic Site,* North Carolina. Washington, 1956.

Priestley, Herbert Ingram, *Tristan de Luna, Conquistador of The Old South; a study of Spanish imperial strategy*. The Arthur H. Clark Co., 1936.

Quattlebaum, Paul, *The Land Called Chicora*. Spartanburg, South Carolina. Reprint Co., 1956.

Quinn, David Beers. *The Roanoke Voyages*. Hakluyt Society, London, 1955.

Quinn, David Beers. *Set Fair For Roanoke*. Univ. of North Carolina Press, Chapel Hill, 1985.

Rowland, Dunbar, *A Symposium on The Place of Discovery of The Mississippi River by Hernando de Soto*. Jackson, Mississippi, 1927.

Schell, Rolfe F. *De Soto Didn't Land at Tampa*. Island Press, Fort Myers Beach, Florida, 1966.

Shea, John Dawson Gilmary. *Catholic Missions Among The Indian Tribes of The United States*. Arno Press, 1969.

Solis de Meras, Gonzalo. *Pedro Menendez de Aviles; Memorial*. University of Florida Press, 1964.

South Carolina Antiquities, Archaeological Society of South Car. Columbia, South Carolina, 1974-1979.

United States De Soto Commission Final Report, House Doc. 71. Washington, D.C., 1939.

Walker, Thomas Dr. *Journal Of An Exploration*. Little Brown and Co., Boston, 1888.

Weare, G.E. Cabot's *Discovery of North America*. John MacQueen, London, 1897.

Williams, Samuel Cole. *Early Travels in The Tennessee Country*. The Watauga Press, Johnson City, Tennessee, 1928.

Winsor, Justin. *Narrative and Critical History of America.* Houghton, Mifflin and Co., Boston, 1884-91.

Zavala, Silvio Arturo, *The Political Philosophy of The Conquest of America.* Editorial Cultura, Mejico, 1953.

Zavala, Silvio Arturo, *New Viewpoints on The Spanish Colonization of America.* University of Penn. Press; H. Milford, London, 1943.

THE MELUNGEONS INDEX

-A-

-B-

-C-

-H-

-J-

-K-

-L-

-M-

-N-

-O-

-P-

-R-

-S-

-T-

-U-

-V-

-W-

-X-